History of Bali

A Captivating Guide to Balinese History and the Impact This Island Has Had on the History of Indonesia and Southeast Asia.

Free Bonus from Captivating History
(Available for a Limited time)

Hi History Lovers!

Now you have a chance to join our exclusive history list so you can get your first history ebook for free as well as discounts and a potential to get more history books for free! Simply visit the link below to join.

Captivatinghistory.com/ebook

Also, make sure to follow us on Facebook, Twitter and Youtube by searching for Captivating History.

Contents

Introduction

The unassuming island of Bali in maritime Southeast Asia is a brilliant jewel in the crown of archipelagic Indonesia, drawing millions of tourists year after year to its magnificent beaches, lush tropical forests, and unique cultural heritage. Known for centuries as "the Island of the Gods," Bali boasts a multitude of temples representing the spirituality of the peoples that have landed on her shores since ancient times. The most intrinsic of these magnificent temples are those dedicated to Balinese Hinduism, an endemic blending of Buddhism, Hinduism, animism, and indigenous beliefs introduced from Java by the Majapahit Empire half a millennia ago.

Bali's mystique and its historical reluctance to submit to foreign powers made her an even brighter jewel, a rare gem that had yet to be snatched by force during the colonial era. After a three-hundred-year-long resistance, the island finally came completely under Dutch suzerainty at the turn of the 20th century, which would be followed shortly afterward by the impact of the world wars and then inevitably the creation of Indonesia as an independent republic.

Whether through breathtaking scenery, the island's World Heritage status for the subak rice irrigation system, a wealth of culture—whether it be music, dancing, or its history of colorful religious pantomimes and parades—or the impact of its ornate ancient temples, Bali still mesmerizes visitors to its shores as it has done since prehistoric times. With a lack of natural resources or the valuable items that maritime traders of old required for gain, it is curious why Bali attracted so much attention and intrigue throughout history. The Balinese talent of morphing to suit the changing times has kept an exceptional and vulnerable culture protected through each successive wave of foreign interference. Bali exists as a living monument to the past, unchanged in many ways and still a refuge for those seeking spiritual and existential solace.

Perhaps the island is simply fortuitously positioned along the arc of the Indonesia island chain, quietly hiding from the real world, but perhaps it was the magical work of an ancient Hindu priest who built strings of sea temples to protect her shores. Whatever has kept Bali resistant to metamorphosis over the ages remains there still, quietly celebrating the beauty and touching story of this extraordinary island.

Chapter 1 – Bali within Indonesia

The history of Bali needs to be understood within the context of its geographical position within Southeast Asia and, more specifically, as a province of the archipelagic nation of the Republic of Indonesia. Indonesia's thirty-four provinces constitute more than seventeen thousand islands that spread in an arc from the Indian to the Pacific Oceans and are bordered by Asia to the north and Oceana (including Australia) to the south. Indonesia is composed entirely of islands and is the largest island country in the world. Indonesia, along with Malaysia, Papua New Guinea, the Philippines, the Solomon Islands, and Timor-Leste, form an oceanic area known as the Coral Triangle. The Coral Triangle is an ecologically significant region of abundant coral and marine life that is recognized as the global center of marine biodiversity conservation. Referred to as the "Amazon of the Seas," the Coral Triangle covers an area of 5.7 million square kilometers of ocean waters that contain almost 80 percent of the world's shallow-water reef-building coral species, almost 40 percent of global reef fishes, most of the world's sea turtles, and other unique marine wonders.

Southeast Asia can be divided into mainland and archipelagic, of which Indonesia is a part of the latter. The mainland of Southeast Asia can be called by the historical name of Indochina, which is essentially a large peninsula consisting of the countries of Cambodia, Laos, Myanmar, Mainland Malaysia, Thailand, and Vietnam. As part of maritime Southeast Asia, the region of islands, including modern-day Indonesia, Malaysia, Singapore, southern Thailand, the Philippines, Brunei, East Timor, and Taiwan, can also be referred to as the Malay Archipelago or by the historical 14th-century name of *Nusantara* ("outer islands"). The word *nusa* is a derivative of this name and means *island*. The Indonesian archipelago has been a valuable area for trade since as early as the 7th century CE when regional empires traded with China and India, being replaced by colonial trading powers from the 1500s onward. European colonial influences were active in Indonesia until as late as the mid-20th century, with the Dutch ultimately being the dominating power in the region for 350 years. The concept of a sovereign Indonesia emerged as late as the early 20th century, with the country gaining independence from all colonial powers in 1945, after the surrender of the Japanese at the end of the Second World War. However, the last remaining colonial influence, the Dutch, would not accept Indonesia's sovereignty until 1949 following an armed conflict.

Indonesia's national motto, *Bhinneka Tunggal Ika* ("Unity in Diversity"), reflects its multitudinous ethnic and linguistic population groupings and the rich cultural diversity for which it is known. While Javanese is the largest linguistic group, the national language is Indonesian—a standardized version of the Austronesian Malay language. Despite Islam being the dominant religion in Indonesia, historical influences of Hinduism, Buddhism, and Christianity have resulted in widespread religious pluralism.

Modern-day Indonesia is constituted of thirty-four provinces divided into seven geographical regions: Sumatra, Java, Kalimantan, Sulawesi, Western New Guinea (Papua), the Maluku Islands, and the Lesser and Greater Sunda Islands. Whereas Sumatra, Java, Kalimantan, Sulawesi, and Western New Guinea are large islands or sections of large islands in their own right, the Sundas and Moluccas are island groupings whose sovereignty is often shared with other Southeast Asian nations. Sumatra is the second largest island (after Kalimantan) of the Indonesian chain, and it extends adjacent to the south of the Malaysian mainland. Java follows the island arc of Sumatra and is not only the most populated island in Indonesia (representing 56 percent of Indonesia's population, over 140 million people) but is also the most populated island in the world. On the northwestern coast of Java, the Indonesian capital of Jakarta is home to almost eleven million people and is the second most populated global urban area after Tokyo. Together with Borneo (most of which consists of Kalimantan) and Sulawesi, these four islands constitute the Greater Sunda Islands. All Indonesian provinces—except Bali, which is predominantly Hindu—are majority Muslim, and it is the most populous Muslim majority country in the world.

The province (*propinsi* or *provinsi*) of Bali is part of the Lesser Sunda Islands. The Lesser Sundas are known in Indonesian as the *Kepulauan Nusa Tenggara* ("Southeastern Archipelago") or the *Kepulauan Sunda Kecil* ("the Lesser Sunda Archipelago"). Together with the four large islands of the Greater Sunda Islands, they make up the Sunda Islands, which are commonly named for and were formed by the volcanic Sunda Arc. The Lesser Sundas extend west-east from the arc of Sumatra and Java, stretching from Bali in the west to the Tanimbar Islands in the east. The Lesser Sundas toward the east also commonly fall under the Indonesian island grouping of the Maluku (Molucca) Islands as well. The Maluku archipelago lies between the Indonesian islands of Sulawesi to the west and New Guinea to the east (and northeast of Timor). The Maluku Islands, as well as a small island grouping to their south called the Banda Islands, were historically referred to as the "Spice Islands" by colonial-era maritime traders due to their natural abundance of nutmeg, mace, and cloves. The island of Bali is not easily navigable since it is surrounded by coral reefs, which made it extremely difficult to approach in times past. The currents that separate Java from Bali to the west are very strong, and the south is often lashed by heavy seas.

The island country of Indonesia is a geological product of the volcanic activity of the Pacific Ring of Fire and possibly other seismic belts. The Ring of Fire is an inverted horseshoe-shaped zone of intense tectonic forces that encapsulates most of the Pacific Ocean and extends in and around Indonesia and most of the archipelagic section of Southeast Asia. The Ring of Fire is associated with persistent and seismic earthquakes and volcanic activity, which are a result of shifting continental plates that lie deep below the ocean's surface within the earth's lithosphere (or outermost solid layer). Globally, there are seven major tectonic plates, as well as a number of smaller plates, that are in a continual and gradual process of movement or drift. The relative motion of plates at the places where they meet creates friction and results in earthquakes and volcanoes and subsequently the formation of mountains or trenches. The Pacific Ring of Fire is specifically marked at its extremities by the process of subduction, whereby two plates push against each other. Through this convergence, one plate is pushed below another, ultimately forcing it to be recycled into the earth's mantle (a deeper, hotter, and more viscous layer of the planet).

The eastern islands of Indonesia (most of the Lesser Sundas except Bali, Sulawesi, the Maluku Islands, and all other landmasses toward the east) are often associated with the Ring of Fire, but there is scientific disagreement as to whether the western islands can be included with the Ring of Fire. These islands are also associated with the Alpide Belt. The Alpide Belt is a seismic zone that stretches from western Southeast Asia along the mountainous regions of southern Eurasia through the extent of Europe to the Atlantic in the west. In geological terms, western Indonesia includes the Greater Sunda Islands, as well as Bali, Lombok, Sumbawa, and Sangeang, which are politically part of the Lesser Sundas.

[2] Lesser Sunda Islands, Indonesia, showing Bali at the far west, adjacent to Java.

Lencer, CC BY-SA 3.0 <https://creativecommons.org/licenses/by-sa/3.0>, via Wikimedia Commons https://commons.wikimedia.org/wiki/File:Lesser_Sunda_Islands_en.png

Regardless of which geological arc Bali is formed, it was the result of tectonic subduction of the Indo-Australian Plate under the Eurasian Plate and the subsequent lifting of the ocean floor above sea level. The deformation of the upper Eurasian Plate has resulted in a string of volcanoes (stratovolcanoes) lying west-east across the northern lands of Bali, although it is not itself a volcanic island. The youngest of Bali's volcanos are the easterly most ones, of which the youngest is Mount Agung, or *Gunung Agung* ("Great Mountain"). It stands at 3,000 meters (close to 10,000 feet) above sea level and remains active.

In general, the soils of Indonesia are subject to deep chemical weathering and rapid erosion because of perpetually high temperatures and heavy precipitation. The tropical rainforest areas experience replenishing cycles of decomposition and nutrient renewal, but these soils are not necessarily ideal for agriculture because once the forests are cleared, the exposed land is subject to significant erosion and mineral leaching. The presence of active volcanoes, such as Agung on Bali, hold the potential for the replenishment of eroded or leached soils since the earth is replaced periodically by volcanic ash, which renews the amount of soil as well as its nutrient value in time. In particular, the rice paddy irrigation systems on Bali transport this nutrient load from higher altitudes to lower altitudes that are being farmed, and so, the nutrient value of volcanic deposits is beneficially used. Balinese farmers have historically regarded volcanoes as homes to fertility goddesses who bring bounty to their fields.

In geophysical terms, Bali is part of the Sunda Shelf, from which the Sunda Islands derive their name. The Sunda Shelf is an extension of the continental shelf (land edge) of Southeast Asia. Interestingly, all the Lesser Sunda Islands east of Bali (from Lombok onward) are not part of the Sunda Shelf, and a steep undersea gradient separates Bali from much of east and southeast Indonesia, which rest upon the adjacent Sahul (Australian) continental shelf. The biogeographical division that separates the landmasses of the Sunda and Sahul Shelves is known as the Wallace Line. This line was identified by the British naturalist and explorer Alfred Russell Wallace in 1859 during his exploration of the East Indies. Wallace (1823–1913 CE) was the co-author of Charles Darwin's *Origin of the Species* and traveled through maritime Southeast Asia in the 19th century, investigating flora and fauna. The line was later given its name by an English biologist and a staunch early supporter of the theory of evolution, Thomas Henry Huxley, who was also born in the 19th century.

The Wallace Line demarcates a distinct difference in fauna and flora between the west and east of this hypothetical boundary according to the continental origins of the landmasses. The western side of the line is distinctly Asian, and the eastern side, also known as Wallacea, is a transitional zone or buffer between Asia and Australia, and it contains a mix of both Asian and Australian species. While this division refers mostly to fauna (animal species), it is also apparently for floral (plant) species as well, although not as specifically. The Wallace Line runs through Indonesia, separating Borneo from

Sulawesi, and most notably through the Lombok Strait, separating Bali from Lombok.

The Sunda Shelf that extends from the Southeast Asian continent is a result of erosion of the main continent and volcanic activity that accumulated and was compacted around the continent's edges over the millennia as sea levels rose and fell through the various ice ages. Sundaland is the name given to the exposed areas of land that were visible during the last ice age (24,000 to 17,000 BCE). This extended Asian landmass included the Malay Peninsula, Borneo, Java, Sumatra, Bali, and other surrounding islands. Around approximately 14,000 BCE, rising meltwater from the end of the last ice age filled the low-lying areas between the islands that are present today. The seas between the islands cover ancient peneplains, which are seismically stable plains in the final stages of fluvial erosion.

The Sunda Shelf is typically characterized by low seismic activity and on the whole is considered stable, except for active volcanoes on Sumatra, Java, and Bali, which are technically an adjunction to the Sunda Shelf known as the Sunda Arc—the volcanic arc created by the subduction of the Indo-Australian and Eurasian Plates. The complicated pattern and history of geological formation on and around the Sunda Shelf and the erratic creation and dissolution of land bridges with the Asian continent have given rise to a high level of biodiversity, as well as a significant degree of biological endemism, including local discontinuities, such as across the Wallace Line. On Bali itself, thick deposits of volcanic ash have created good soil fertility and resulted in agricultural prosperity for the islands. The Balinese islands were once connected to Java during low sea levels in the various ice ages, and their fauna and flora are distinctly Asian.

Of Indonesia's approximately 270 million people, 1.5 percent (more than four million people) resided in provincial Bali in 2019. The province of Bali is constituted of four islands: Bali, Nusa Penida, Nusa Lembongan, and Nusa Ceningan, covering a land area of almost six thousand square kilometers (0.3 percent of the land area of

Indonesia). The capital of Bali—Denpasar—lies to the south and is home to more than 90 percent of the provincial population in its greater metropolitan area. The three smaller islands are clustered to the southeast. The main island of Bali is what is commonly referred to as Bali in historical and contemporary terms and has been the location for the rise and fall of the events of the provincial archipelagic cluster. Bali is divided into eight administrative regencies (*kabupaten*), as well as the city (*kota*) of Denpasar. The eight regions are Badung, Bangli, Buleleng, Gianyar, Jembrana, Karangasem, Klungkung, and Tabanan. Klungkung includes Bali's three small satellite islands. Each of these regencies has its own local government and legislative body. These *kabupaten* developed during the 17th-century rulership of Bali when its single monarchy began separating into distinctive kingdoms. Although historically there were nine kingdoms, the eight resulting regencies have largely kept the boundaries that can be seen today.

More than 80 percent of Bali practices the Hindu religion today, with 12 percent being Muslim, 5 percent Christian, and 0.5 percent Buddhist. Ethnically, most of Bali are indigenous Balinese, with the remaining population constituting other Indonesian ethnicities. Since much of Bali is mountainous—essentially, it is a continuation of the central mountain chain of Java—most of the population of Bali is centered toward the south of the island on the lowlands. The combination of the climate, the mountainous north, and volcanic soils have made for an exceptionally rich agricultural heritage, and rice fields cover the southward-descending slopes that lead to the sea. The northward-descending slopes of Bali that face the Java Sea are steeper and used for coffee plantations. Unlike the less populated areas of Indonesia, where indigenous vegetation consists mostly of broadleaf evergreen forests, most of the vegetation on Java and Bali is dominated by cultivated plants. The remaining indigenous areas are characterized by hilly tropical rainforests. The coastal vegetation of Bali consists mostly of mangroves, mangrove palms, and swamp forests in locations where there are no beaches, human habitation, or other development. The mountainous areas of Bali consist of alpine and subalpine vegetation.

Certain fauna and flora are endemic or sacred to the Balinese, such as the rare Balinese climbing bamboo and the sacred frangipani flower. The Balinese tiger, now believed to be extinct, once roamed the western forests. Leopards and macaque monkeys are still found in Bali, and teak and giant banyan trees are amongst Bali's coveted arboreal treasures. Deer and wild pigs roam freely on the island. On Java, the endemic Javanese peacocks and single-horned Javan rhinoceros can be found, although the rhinoceros are critically endangered and mostly contained within wildlife preserves. The endangered and protected orangutan primate is native to Borneo and Sumatra. Overall, Indonesia is home to forty thousand species of flowering plants (including five thousand species of orchids). Like the fauna of Indonesia, many of these species are unique to the region and sometimes endemic to the specific island(s) on which they occur. Indonesia is home to three thousand species of trees, which are often used for indigenous or commercial purposes. These trees include ironwood, sandalwood, woody rattan, and others that produce unique fruits, nuts, and other beneficial products.

The Ubud Monkey Forest, Bali.

Bali is the westernmost island of the Lesser Sunda Islands, lying just 3.2 kilometers (2 miles) east of Java, separated by the Bali Strait. To the east of Bali, Lombok lies twenty kilometers (about twelve miles) away across the Lombok Strait. Bali lies about eight degrees south of the equator and experiences a tropical climate with little distinction between seasons in terms of temperature. It averages around 30 degrees Celsius (86 degrees Fahrenheit) with high humidity year-round. The wet monsoon season from October to April usually brings heavy rains, particularly from December to March. The main island is approximately 150 kilometers wide and 110 kilometers long from north to south and is home to 99 percent of Bali's population. Over the last fifty years, Bali has become an increasingly popular tourist destination and draws people from around the world to its pristine forests and beaches, unique fauna, rich coral reefs as part of the Coral Triangle, cultural heritage, and cosmopolitan nightlife. The island of Bali draws at least 80 percent of its economy from tourism-related businesses and is the main Indonesian tourist destination. The

Balinese way of life is deeply spiritual, aesthetic, and cultural, with worship, dance, and other art forms being the most important part of life on the island.

Chapter 2 – Bali before the Common Era

One of the first known specimens of *Homo erectus* (upright humans but before modern man) were found on Java, dating from between one million and 700,000 years ago. Similarly, paleolithic evidence (dating from 1,000,000 to 200,000 BCE) has been found on Bali, indicating that it was also inhabited by very early man during this time. Ancient tools such as hand axes were found in the villages of Sembiran and Trunyan in the north and northeast of the main island, respectively. Further evidence of *Homo erectus* exists in Bali from the Mesolithic period (200,000-30,000 BCE). This later evidence suggests more advanced peoples who used more sophisticated tools such as arrow points and tools made of animal bones. These Mesolithic peoples lived in temporary caves such as those found in the Pecatu hills of the Badung regency. The first sign of modern man (*Homo sapiens*) began in about 45,000 BCE as continental people migrated south from the mainland and began replacing *Homo erectus*.

The presence of Paleolithic and Mesolithic man on Java and Bali suggests that the islands were more accessible during certain periods in history, like the ice ages when sea levels were lower and when land bridges existed between areas that are now islands divided by the sea. By the Neolithic period (starting in about 10,000 BCE), sea levels had risen to produce the arrangement of islands we know as Indonesia in the present era. Humankind also developed the maritime navigation skills and technologies (boats) to move from the mainland to these islands, as well as between the islands. But the early peoples of the Neolithic period most importantly relied on nature for this migration, specifically, ocean currents, tides, and winds, and, most importantly for Southeast Asia, the seasonal monsoons.

The concept of a monsoon is prevalent throughout the tropics and is most commonly associated with wet weather. However, monsoons refer to wind, specifically to a seasonal change in the direction of the prevailing (strongest) winds of a region. A monsoon season can bring dry or wet conditions throughout the tropics, depending on the direction from which the wind is blowing. Monsoons traveling overseas, particularly warm seas, will bring wet weather. Monsoons traveling overland will bring drier weather. Monsoons blow from colder to warmer regions, and these winds determine the climate for most of Southeast Asia. Technically, summer monsoon winds blow from the southwest during June to September, and winter monsoon winds, or trade winds, blow from the northeast from October to March.

However, this general pattern of monsoon winds is attributed to the Northern Hemisphere, and most of Indonesia, specifically Bali, are within the Southern Hemisphere (but only slightly within the Southern Hemisphere). Local weather patterns, including the specific arrangement of larger islands near Bali (such as Sumatra), also affect its experience of monsoon weather and create anomalies in the island from experiencing a typical tropical monsoon weather pattern. Although Bali's true wet season is in its summer (October to March), since it is so close to the equator, it can experience year-round rains brought by alternating monsoon winds. Sir Stamford Raffles, a British statesman and governor of the Dutch East Indies in the early 19th century who wrote *The History of Java* (published in 1817), noted that all of the Southeast Asian countries situated within ten degrees of the equator experienced "one eternal summer" that is not distinguished by hot and cold but by wet (hot and rainy) and dry (hot and humid) weather. The humidity and torrential rain of Bali's wet monsoon season (December to March) are critical for agriculture. The wet monsoon season is essential for much of Southeast Asia since many of these countries do not have extensive natural or manmade irrigation or damming systems, either near their croplands or underground in the form of deep aquifers. The wet monsoons provide necessary water for both livestock and crop farming.

Historically, early exploration is considerably attributed to monsoon wind patterns in Southeast Asia. However, the ancient monsoon winds did not specifically follow modern calendars because of the earth's axial precession. Both early migratory peoples and ancient trade mariners used monsoon wind patterns to discover and explore new lands. Monsoon winds and their associated currents were essential in assisting ancient cultures to navigate their small, indigenous seafaring crafts to foreign lands, such as the Indonesian archipelago, which was only accessible via sea. Recent archaeological evidence along the coasts of Southeast Asia, India, and the Middle East provides persuasive evidence of a network of mariners in ancient times, dating to approximately two millennia before the Common Era, roughly around the time that Bali began to be settled.

The monsoon winds of Southeast Asia altered the surface currents of its seas and oceans to enable smaller craft to navigate along the maritime trade routes. Since ancient sailing and rowing vessels were smaller and either powered by sails or people, they relied mostly on the direction of the prevailing winds to set their direction. Much of Southeast Asia began being populated sometime between 6,500 BCE and 4,500 BCE (the Neolithic period) by the Austronesian peoples. The Austronesians are an ethnically and linguistically related people who originated from mainland Asia. There is one popular historical theory that suggests Austronesians migrated via Taiwan to populate maritime Southeast Asia, but another suggests Austronesian migration patterns originated from Indonesia/Wallacea (of which Bali is a part). Regardless of the various theories of the initial migratory patterns of this ethnic group, the mainland origins of the Austronesians were most likely mainland southern China and mainland northern Southeast Asia. The preexistence of archaic settled tribes throughout mainland southern Asia meant that natural population expansion moved southward and into maritime Southeast Asia, Oceana, and the Indian and Pacific Oceans.

Archaeological evidence, such as linguistics, human and animal DNA, ocean voyaging technology, and pottery, has been used to link approximately 350 million people currently living in Madagascar, Southeast Asia (and, in part, within mainland Asia), Oceana (including areas of mainland Australia), and the Pacific islands with a common genetic source. Known as the Austronesian peoples, it is thought that they moved from southern mainland China and either through Taiwan or Indonesia (or both) in an outward expansion over thousands of years. Although different evidence points to different potentials for the spread of the Austronesian peoples, they share commonalities that indicate the hereditary sharing of knowledge and resources. Some of this indigenous knowledge included ocean voyaging technologies, such as ocean sailing canoes, farming methods like the irrigated rice terraces, domesticated animals like wild pigs and chickens, and cultivated plants like taro, banana, breadfruit, and sugarcane. Since the Austronesians' staple food source was rice, they are most commonly associated with the complex irrigation systems still evident today in much of Southeast Asia. These cascading rice paddies (fields) are known in Bali as the subak system.

The modern-day family of languages spoken in much of the Indonesian archipelago is part of the 1,200 contemporary Austronesian languages. The Austronesian language group covers a vast maritime geographical area and includes about 20 percent of the world's languages. The Austronesian expansion was most likely the result of growing population numbers reliant on new lands for cultivation, which would have been exacerbated by resource-poor small islands and the necessity to continue expanding. It is also likely that many of the new lands discovered by the Austronesian peoples were uninhabited or sparsely inhabited, allowing for the development of new, independent settlements or, in some cases, cross-pollination of ethnicities.

The Austronesian peoples were thought to have begun inhabiting Bali and its surrounding islands in approximately the second millennium BCE. The tools discovered in Bali include rectangular adzes (work axes) and agricultural tools, as well as red-slipped decorated pottery. The early Austronesian settlers cleared rainforests for their villages, and they made plaited crafts as well as boats. They ate pork and chewed betel—a peppery vine with cultural value. Like many early people of Bali, the Austronesians settled mostly in the mountainous regions of the island. They buried some of their dead (possibly of higher social status) in unusual and distinctive oval stone sarcophagi. The sarcophagi were decorated with human head illustrations or zoomorphic figures, and because the sarcophagi were small and pod-like, the bodies sometimes had to be folded into three to fit in the coffins. These coffins were used into the Bronze Age (up to the first millennium BCE).

There is evidence of bronze and iron metallurgy on the Southeast Asian islands occurring in about 500 BCE, which is believed to be more than that simply traded with other regions. Dong Son drums were also traded at this time from Vietnam to the Sunda and surrounding islands. Indian pottery dating from circa 200 BCE to 200 CE has been unearthed in Bali and Java, proving Bali was part of ancient trading routes with greater Asia. It is likely that by 500 CE, Southeast Asia was the site of prolific inter- and intra-regional trade, but it is also likely that one of the main sources of this burgeoning life—Taiwan—became increasingly removed from Nusantara life. Rising sea levels since the end of the last ice age meant that the sea-crossings that may have been manageable in the millennia that initiated Austronesian expansion were growing wider and were possibly climatically more dangerous to navigate.

The Austronesian explorers were thought to have used outrigger canoes and proas to navigate to new lands. Unfortunately, these conclusions are drawn mostly upon the indigenous vessels used by the Austronesian peoples of today, as well as reports by the early European explorers. It is supposed that most of the evidence of early sailing vessels has been destroyed by the climatic conditions of the tropics and the erosive and destructive effects of the ocean. It is also possible that early colonists destroyed indigenous vessels in order to hold the native peoples captive on the islands and, therefore, more under their control.

Outrigger vessels are those where the hull is supported by a lateral stabilizing force such as a second float, and a proa (or a prau) is a type of multi-hulled (usually double) outrigger sailboat. These watercraft inventions, as well as others, were the most important technologies of the Austronesian peoples and were what enabled them to cover significant distances of the oceans and colonize vast tracts of Southeast Asia and the Pacific.

An example of a "flying" (very fast) proa with a crab-claw sail. These multi-hulled outrigger sailboats of the Austronesian peoples may have been used to explore new lands. Similar craft are used by Austronesian people to this day.

https://commons.wikimedia.org/wiki/File:Proa_(PSF).png

Stone tools dating from approximately 2500 to 2000 BCE have been discovered in Cekik on the western end of Bali (modern-day Gilimanuk). Also at Cekik, as well as inland at Sembiran, indications of a Bronze Age people dating from the 3rd century BCE have been discovered. Evidence from these sites reveals communities of fishermen, hunters, and farmers. It is evident that these early peoples of Bali had knowledge of metallurgy and acquired the skills to cast or smelt copper, bronze, and iron. These Bronze Age peoples are thought to have originated from Indochina, specifically the Dong Son area of Vietnam, and brought metals and metallurgy skills with them. The Dong Son Bronze Age culture was named after a village of northern Vietnam (the Red River Valley) and existed from approximately one millennium before the Common Era to about the 1st century of the Common Era.

The Dong Son were themselves originally believed to have migrated from the southern Chinese mainland to northern Vietnam, bringing their farming (specifically rice cultivation) and metallurgy techniques with them. Although the Dong Son were also skilled in ironwork and carried traditional cultural Chinese artifacts with them, they are best known for their pervasive and high-quality bronze kettle drums. Dong Son religious stone monuments were also a mark of their culture and are similar to those found in Polynesia. Like all Austronesian peoples, the Dong Son were great seafarers who traveled and traded throughout Southeast Asia and whose people naturally chose to settle in certain parts of the various archipelagos. There is evidence that Balinese people acquired the Dong Son metallurgical techniques between the 8th and 3rd centuries BCE. Although the raw materials to make bronze (copper and tin) needed to be imported, it seems that the Balinese had acquired the skills to both mold and decorate tools, weapons, jewelry, and drums.

The development of the Indonesian Pejeng drum was an early 1st and 2nd century CE adaptation of the Dong Son kettle drum. They are one of the region's finest examples of localized metalworking. The Pejeng drums were named after the Bronze Age village of Pejeng in Bali. These drums differed from traditional Dong Son drums in that they were longer and were cast in two pieces using wax molds. These drums were produced extensively on the islands of Java and Bali during the first millennium CE.

The Balinese variation, specifically, is one of the most sophisticated artifacts of Indonesia's prehistory. The finest example of the Pejeng drum is the Moon of Pejeng, the largest example of its kind in the world and currently on display at the temple of Pura Penataran Sasih in Pejeng near Ubud (southwest Gianyar). The Moon of Pejeng is considered highly sacred by the local people and is thought to have been an important relic of early rice cultivation rituals. The village of Pejeng lies in the Petauan River valley, which, along with its neighbor the Pakerisan River valley, forms the epicenter of the southern Balinese region of earliest rice cultivation. These complex irrigated rice fields are the most important inherited origins of early Balinese peoples.

The six-foot-long (187-centimeter-long) Pejeng Moon drum is thought to have been carved about three hundred years before the Common Era. Balinese legends tell that the drum was originally one of the wheels of a chariot that pulled the real moon through the night sky. One night, the wheel broke from the chariot and fell to the earth in a tree in Pejeng. The wheel shone as brightly as the moon and was extinguished and cooled by a passing thief who climbed the tree and urinated on it! The thief paid for this sacrilege with his life, but the drum was kept as a sacred relic by the villagers.

Top: Neolithic (6,500– 4,500 BCE) stone sarcophagus, Bali Museum.

Bpttom: A Pejeng kettle drum dating from the 1ˢᵗ-2ⁿᵈ Century CE.

Archaeological discoveries in Bali suggest that human settlement before the Common Era happened in stages but that these migrations were limited and independent of one another. Maritime Southeast Asia is known to be a melting pot of cultures, specifically Indonesia, which boasts a mix of an estimated 250 ethnic groups. Bali is similar in the diversity of its ethnic origins. Contemporary ethnicities in Bali are a unique genetic blend of Chinese, Malay, Polynesian, Melanesian (Pacific peoples), Indian, and Javanese. However, it was the arrival of Hindu merchants from the 1ˢᵗ century CE and onward that made the most significant impact on the population expansion of ancient Bali.

Chapter 3 – The Historic Period

Much of the ancient and historical movements of people through time have arisen from common interests regarding trade. The Austronesian peoples were some of the first to create a maritime trade network across the Indo-Pacific. They traded seacraft, paan (an end product of the betel leaf, like chewing tobacco), and cultivars crucial to farming, such as coconuts, bananas, and sugarcane. Trade networks such as these connected dominant material cultures like India and China. As early Austronesian trade increased, spices became the main imports moving from east to west, surpassing other commodities and products. These early forerunners of the global spice trade eventually developed into the Maritime Silk Road—the multicultural trade network that connected Africa, Europe, China, Southeast Asia, the Indian subcontinent, and the Arabian Peninsula from the 2nd century BCE until the 15th century CE.

India's connection to Southeast Asia was extremely important to the merchants of Arabia and Persia (Iran) in the 7th and 8th centuries. However, by the 11th century CE, the expansive Muslim Seljuk Empire blocked the route of commodities west and instigated the medieval Crusades. The Seljuk Empire was a vast medieval hegemony that stretched from the Levant in the west to the Hindu Kush in the east, and it was bordered by the Persian Gulf in the south and included most of central Asia. Similarly, the Ottoman Empire negatively impacted the spice trade in the mid-1400s, igniting the age of maritime discovery and European colonization as voyages left Europe and rounded the continents in search of commodities. Spices produced in Near and Far Eastern countries, such as cinnamon, clove, turmeric, cassia, cardamom, ginger, and pepper, were in high demand to nations on the ancient spice route. The "Spice Islands" of Indonesia (the Maluku or Molucca Islands and the Banda Islands) were kept secret by the traders, and they developed fantastical tales about the source of the spices to protect these commodities.

The historical period of Bali stretches from the start of the Common Era until the Majapahit Empire in 1343, although it was most active from approximately the seventh millennium of the Common Era. The greatest influences in that time were from influxes of people from India, Java, and China. The Austronesian and Dong Son peoples constituted the original settlers of Bali. The next significant group was approximately four hundred people who moved from eastern Java, more specifically the village of Aga, in about the 8th century CE. They settled in the remote mountainous area around the volcano named Gunung Agung ("Great Mountain"), believing that mountainous areas brought them closer to the gods. These Aga communities prospered and remain a significant Balinese population group today. However, the Bali Agas' strictly preserved cultural code means that, to this day, their communities remain separate and isolated from much of Balinese life, particularly that familiar to modern-day tourists.

Aspects of Aga life, such as clothing and architecture, have been retained through the centuries. For example, the ancient and traditional geringsing fabric unique to the Bali Aga village of Tenganan Pegringsingan is made using an ancient technique of color dyeing or the double ikat method (a form of tie-dyeing). The geringsing fabrics are black, red (rust), and neutral, and they are considered sacred by the Bali Aga, particularly when it comes to healing. "Gering" means illness, and "sing" means no. The geringsing are often ascribed supernatural powers and are patterned with Hindu motifs or other inspirational cultural patterns, such as the frangipani flower (*jepun*). Geringsing are used extensively for cultural and religious ceremonies within Tenganan Pegringsingan village life. References to geringsing exist within ancient Javanese literature and Buddhist poetry. The 1365 poem *Nagarakretagama* (*Nagarakrtagama, Desawarnana,* or *Desavarnana*), written by the Buddhist sage Mpu Prapanca, describes curtains of the infamous Javanese Majapahit ruler Hayam Wuruk as being made of geringsing.

Tenganan (Bali Aga) women wearing the geringsing-patterned cloth.

The most pervasive and lasting influence of population influx for ancient Bali was by peaceful Indian traders who began arriving on the island in the 1ˢ century CE. The traders are thought to have been from southern India and Sri Lanka, and they moved simultaneously into Indochina and southern China. These Indian mercantile spiritualists would most likely have largely settled in Java—Bali's closest, largest, and most resource-laden island neighbor—before moving across to Bali. From the historical period onward, Java's and Bali's histories have been inextricably linked.

The Indian merchants introduced both Hinduism and Buddhism to Bali. Hinduism was an ancient way of life that had been practiced on the Indian subcontinent since before the second millennium BCE. Buddhism, which was founded in the late 6th century BCE, was becoming entrenched as a world religion at the time, spreading throughout Asia and Southeast Asia along the trade routes. Mahayana Buddhism was brought to Bali, which is one of the two main branches of ancient Buddhism. This branch is the less traditionalist branch of Buddhism (as opposed to Theravada Buddhism) and is the most widely practiced form of the religion today.

The first written records discovered in Bali were Buddhist inscriptions on clay tablets, which were discovered inside stone Buddhist stupas, or ceremonial containers, known as stupikas. These votive writings, which date from the 8th century CE, were found in villages in the regency of Gianyar. Along with the stupikas, which indicate the presence of Buddhism in Bali, the Blanjong Pillar (*Prasasti Blanjong* or Belanjong Pillar) was discovered in the southern area of Sanur and is dated exactly to 914 CE. The low stone pillar is inscribed using both the old Balinese language and Indian Sanskrit, and it mentions King Sri Kesari of Bali, who commissioned the pillar. Three other inscriptions mentioning King Kesari were discovered in central Bali, which indicates there was some regional struggle that required him to enforce his territory. King Kesari is the first known Balinese king to use the title Warmadewa (Varmadeva). Evidence of this title for the next century suggests kings that were linked in a monarchical sense, but there is insufficient evidence to confirm if Warmadewa refers to a biological dynasty or not. The most recent and final appearance of the title Warmadewa is on an inscription attributed to the well-known King Udayana Warmadewa, dated 1011 CE. King Udayana's most important historical claim is as the father of the renowned King Airlangga, who ruled Java from around 1020 to

1040 CE. The title Warmadewa was not seen again, and it is thought to have disappeared as Javanese expansion and rule expanded and overtook Bali.

The name "Bali" is believed to have originated in about the 7th century CE, although written evidence of its name dates from a little later. *Bali dwipa* ("Bali Island") was discovered in several inscriptions, including the Blanjong Pillar. The name "Bali" is thought to be derived from the word *bebali*, meaning "offerings," and spread by way of eastern Java through Hindu spiritualism and the concept of making donations to the spirit world, such as flowers, food, cloth, and decorations. Offerings are a core part of Balinese spirituality to this day, and the multitude of temples and sacred sites of the island are continually adorned with gifts to spirits and gods.

A concentration of archaeological finds in the Balinese regency of Gianyar suggests that this region may have been a political, religious, and cultural capital during the 10th and 11th centuries of the Common Era. At the same time, Shaivite (Shivaite) Hinduism was taking hold in Bali. Shaivism is one of the main Hindu traditions, in which Shiva is worshiped as the supreme being. It is one of the largest sects of Hinduism and is believed to be the oldest living religion in the world. The 11th-century stone-carved Elephant Cave (Goa Gajah) near Ubud and the adjoining bathing place are testimony to the Warmadewa kings' adherence to Buddhism as well as Shaivite Hinduism since the temple complex contains evidence of both religions in its stone carvings. A menacing figure has been carved at the entrance to the cave, which leads to a small chamber, assumed for meditation. Nearby, a bathing pool was carved out of stone and lined with seven stone women pouring water from pitchers into the pool.

King Udayana Warmadewa ruled Bali in the second half of the 10th century. At the same time, the Medang Kingdom of Java was flourishing. The Medang, also known as the Mataram, Kingdom was a sophisticated Hindu-Buddhist monarchy ruled by the Indianized Shailendra (Sailendra, Syailendra, or Selendra) dynasty. In Sanskrit,

Shailendra means "King of the Mountain," and the emergence of the dynasty in the 700s CE in central Java began a cultural renaissance for Bali's closest and most influential island neighbor. During their approximate 300-year-long rule (from the mid-7th century to the early 11th century CE), the Shailendra dynasty's rulers filled Java with religious monuments, which were mostly Mahayana Buddhist. The Shailendras were a thalassocracy (a seaborne rulership), and most of their focus was on the intra- and inter-trade relationships of Southeast Asia. The Shailendras may have been more than the rulers of the Medang dynasty and could also possibly have been an important part of the Srivijaya Kingdom of Sumatra as well.

King Sri Kesari, who left the inscription on the Belanjong pillar, is thought to have been of Shailendra descent and could possibly have migrated to Bali from Java for the express purpose of establishing a Mahayana Buddhist government in Bali. The title Warmadewa could mean a connection to the Shailendra dynasty. The Medang Kingdom of Java flourished between approximately the 8th and 11th centuries, and it eventually spread to dominate eastern Java, thus moving ever closer as an influential power over Bali. This refined civilization focused heavily on rice farming and then later maritime trade. It was rich in spirituality, arts, and culture, and significant population growth and economic prosperity saw the Medang Kingdom spread to influence Sumatra, Bali, southern Thailand, and other areas of Indochina, as well as parts of the Philippines in time.

Eventually, the Medang Kingdom split into two warring factions, which alternately supported either Buddhism or Hindu Shaivism. The dynasties that headed up these factions were the Shivaist dynasty of Java and the Buddhist dynasty of the Srivijaya Kingdom of Sumatra. In 1006 CE, the Shailendra clan of the Srivijaya Kingdom triumphed when one of their vassals—King Wurawari of Lwaram—conquered the Shivaist capital of Watugaluh in eastern Java. Although the Srivijaya dynasty rose up to become the hegemonic empire of the region, lasting until the 14ᵗʰ century, the Shivaist dynasty continued and had reclaimed eastern Java by 1019.

King Udayana Warmadewa of Bali married an eastern Javanese woman, Queen Mahendradatta of the Isyana dynasty. The Isyana dynasty was the eastern Javanese arm of the Medang Kingdom and proceeded the Sanjaya dynasty of the same geographical region. The first ruler of the Isyanas (or the last ruler of the Sanjayas), Mpu Sindok, had initiated the establishment of rulership in the east of Java in 929 CE. Historical records are confusing, but the Hindu Sanjaya dynasty, which was established in central Bali, could have been an independent kingdom or could have been part of the Shailendras. Either way, they gave way to the Isyanas, and their seat of power was relocated to eastern Java for reasons that are not clear.

The Sanjaya dynasty was founded in approximately 732 CE by King Sanjaya, who was one of the rulers of Medang. Five more kings followed Sanjaya until the eastward migration of the royal court and the establishment of Sindok's Isyana dynasty. Contrary historical records suggest that the Sanjayas and the Shailendras were interwoven and possibly related but were also at odds with one another, competing for dominance in religion and economics throughout Java and farther afield. Some historians deny the existence of the Sanjayas altogether and state that they were merely another branch of the Shailendras. Ironically, the legendary rivalry between the Buddhist Shailendra dynasty and the Hindu Sanjayas is supposed to have led to the establishment of two of the most famous and beautiful temples in Java: the Hindu Prambanan temple and the Buddhist Borobudur.

The marriage of King Udayana and Queen Mahendradatta is evidence of a historical link between the islands of Java and Bali. Queen Mahendradatta was the sister of the last king of the Medang Kingdom, Dharmawangsa (r. 990–1016 CE). These royal siblings claimed a direct lineage from Mpu Sindok as part of the Isyana dynasty. Since Dharmawangsa was supposed to have conquered Bali at some point in his reign, it is likely that the marriage of his sister to

King Udayana was some kind of a strategic arrangement, albeit a loose one. The children produced from this union rose to rule eastern Java as well as Bali. Marakata Pangkaja and later Anak Wungcu (Wungsu) ascended the Balinese throne.

The eldest son of King Udayana and Queen Mahendradatta, Airlangga (or Erlangga), went on to establish the Kahuripan Kingdom of Java that arose after eastern Java's destruction by Wurawari. Airlangga was the only monarch to rule during the brief Kahuripan era of Java. He was born in Bali but crossed over to rule Java (his name meaning "jumping water"), and he was a descendent of both the Isyana and Warmadewa lineages. Certain apocryphal records suggest that Airlangga was born in Java to a different father than King Udayana. It is possible that both Airlangga and his mother, Mahendradatta, first crossed to Bali for her marriage to King Udayana. Airlangga may not have been the son of a Balinese king at all, and the fact that he was not first in line to the Balinese throne might corroborate his illegitimacy to the Balinese royal house. Airlangga was also sent back to his uncle, King Dharmawangsa, in his teenage years to be educated in the eastern Javanese royal court. He was betrothed to his cousin, a daughter of his uncle Dharmawangsa.

During this period, Bali may have been under the direct rule of the Medang Kingdom, which continued to be at war with the Srivijayas of central Java and Sumatra. The invasion of the eastern Javanese capital in 1006 by Wurawari includes a local legend that it occurred on Airlangga's wedding day and that he was the only one left alive, at sixteen years of age, after his entire family was slaughtered. After living as a hermit in the western jungle, by 1019, Airlangga had accumulated loyal allies, made peace with Srivijaya, and established his new kingdom of eastern Java, Kahuripan. Although Kahuripan thrived under the fair and equality-minded Airlangga, there were complications with the succession that saw the disintegration of his hard-fought-for kingdom.

Both of Airlangga's brothers (or half-brothers) who went on to rule Bali, Marakata Pangkaja and Anak Wungcu, were mentioned in historical Balinese inscriptions, and they were evidently fair and charitable leaders. Balinese inscriptions at that time were made on copper slit drums (*tongtong* or *kulkul*). By the 12th century CE, the descendants of Airlangga, Jayasakti (r. 1146–1151) and Jayapangus (r. 1178–1181), went on to rule Bali. Archaeological discoveries have been made of Jayasakti's *Prasasti Desa Depaa* copper plate inscriptions, as well as King Jayapangus's copper plate inscriptions regarding governance and taxes, which were written in the old Balinese script.

Bali's connection to China remained strong throughout the Javanese historical period. Chinese coins, or *Kepeng*, had been in use on the island since the 7th century CE. King Jayapangus (also known as Dalem Balingkang) married a Chinese princess, Tjin We, and the royal couple has been immortalized through the Barong Landung art form. The traditional Balinese Barong is closely linked with Chinese mythological creatures. The Barong is a lion-like creature, and as king of the spirit world, he is heralded as the ultimate victor in the never-ending battle of good versus evil in Balinese mythology. The Barong Landung is a cultural event and oral tradition that celebrates the long-held Balinese-Chinese association. It is a procession of people, music, and effigies that tells a legendary tale of the king and his Chinese queen. Furthermore, the names of several Balinese villages have Chinese words as their root.

Legends, specifically the Barong Landung, suggest that Jayapangus's marriage was without children, so at some point in history, the Warmadewa lineage died out. It is possible that a series of indigenous kings ruled the island in an interim period, which lasted more than a hundred years before the rise of Majapahit. Bali's formal connection to Java remained dormant, but its autonomy was shattered in 1284 by King Kertanegara of the Singhasari Empire. The Singhasari Empire was a 13th-century eastern Javanese stronghold and one of the Hindu-Buddhist Indianized kingdoms of ancient Southeast Asia. Historical Javanese sources tell that King Kertanegara invaded and overcame Bali, capturing the queen and forcing her to appear before the Javanese court. At this point, Bali became part of the Singhasari Empire. The preceding peace of several centuries gave way to Kertanegara's short eight-year-long rule. After he was assassinated during a rebellion, his empire fell. Bali enjoyed another interim period of independence. However, Bali's annexation by Java was renewed, this time with more vigor than in previous generations. King Kertanegara's son, the renowned Vijaya (Raden Wijaya), took the throne and founded the Majapahit Empire in 1293, which was to have a long and lasting influence over Bali.

Chapter 4 – The Majapahit Empire

The Majapahit Empire (also known as the Wilwatikta Empire) was an Indianized kingdom based in central and eastern Java that lasted from approximately the end of the 13th century to the 1500s. Its decline coincided with the rise of Islam in Nusantara, specifically falling to the Islamic Sultanate of Demak of northern Java in 1527. The origins of Majapahit are unclear, although it was mentioned in ancient Javanese and Chinese historical records, particularly in Javanese religious records such as scriptural religious poems. Majapahit was considered a regional superpower of its time. The previous Singhasari Empire had given way to the Majapahit Empire, although the same ruling family—the Rajasa dynasty—continued to rule through the duration of both empires. The Majapahit Empire was a thalassocracy that subsequently developed a highly organized cultural and artistic society that was also economically productive, specifically in regard to rice cultivation. It was considered the last of the great Malay Archipelago Hindu kingdoms before colonial interference, and it is still heralded as one of Indonesia's greatest states, continuing to influence political rulership and identity in Indonesia in the modern day.

The golden age of Majapahit was marked by the rulership of Hayam Wuruk, who reigned from circa 1350 to 1389. During this era, the Majapahit Empire dominated large swathes of Indonesia, including Java, Bali, the southern Malay Peninsula, Borneo and Kalimantan, Sumatra, and the Philippines. The Majapahit coat of arms was the Surya Majapahit, or the Sun of the Majapahit, an emblem resembling a sun or a compass that has been found in many of the Majapahit ruins. A few generations into the Majapahit Empire, Hayam Wuruk, the grandson of the Majapahit founder, Vijaya, legitimately ascended the throne at the age of sixteen. Hayam Wuruk was also known as Rajasanagara. During Hayam Wuruk's rule, the Majapahit Empire dispatched with some of the last remaining maritime empires of the Malay Archipelago to emerge as the dominant thalassocracy in command of much of western and central maritime Southeast Asia.

At home on eastern Java, Majapahit society was refined, wealthy, and cultured. The Hindu court had developed a sophisticated system of religious rituals that became interwoven with everyday life and customs. The divisions between livelihood, religion, art, literature, spirituality, and community were significantly blurred to produce a unique blend of morals, beliefs, and behaviors, which created the foundation for Balinese life as it exists in modern times. The level of influence of the Majapahit Empire over its dominions is a matter of historical debate. Some historians propose more of a royal monopoly on trade and multiple vassal states rather than any form of interference or governance across the archipelagos. Since the empire also developed relationships with outlying countries, such as China and Indochina (Southeast Asian mainland), it is most likely that it held the most control over the islands closest to Java and its capital in eastern Java, Wilwatikta (modern-day Trowulan), and the least control the farther afield its empire stretched.

Around the same time the Majapahit Empire was founded, Muslim traders and proselytizers began entering the archipelagic regions of which Bali was a part, and eventually, sultanates were formed. After the death of Hayam Wuruk in 1389, the Majapahit Empire saw squabbles over succession for the next 130 years until 1519. The disintegration of the dynasty could not withstand the rising power of the Islamic Malacca Sultanate. After a series of battles with the Javanese Sultanate of Demak (part of Muslim Malacca centered on the Malay Peninsula), the Majapahit Empire was finally defeated by 1527. Demak had been one of the first Muslim sultanates to be formed with the newly Islamized Malay Archipelago in the 1400s. Many Majapahit nobles and courtiers moved south from the capital of Majapahit (modern-day Trowulan in Java) to Kediri, also in Java. Shortly after the fall of Majapahit, all of Java came under the control of the Islamic sultanate centered in northern Java, at Demak. Many religious and spiritual people (both Hindu and Buddhist), artisans, royalty and courtiers, and other literati, intelligentsia, and artists moved eastward to Bali rather than submit to a foreign religious and cultural power. In this way, although the formal rulership of the Majapahit era in Bali may have lasted for over two hundred years, the vanquished empire continued to significantly influence Bali until the mid-19th century (and beyond) with the advent of the island's modern historical period and pronounced Dutch intervention.

Abundant evidence of the culture brought across from Majapahit stills exists in Bali today. The split gateway entrances (*candi bentar*), so reminiscent of eastern Java, adorn most of the Balinese temples from this era. The Majapahit architects mastered the use of stone and, more uniquely, of brick for their temples (*puras*) and shrines (*candis*). (The Majapahit red-brick candis may be visited in Bali today.) The Majapahits, like the Balinese in later times, venerated the death of loved ones and great people, and they celebrated the occasion with great pomp and ceremony, often continuing decades after the event. For funerals and religious ceremonies of all kinds, the people of the Majapahit Empire employed the work of artisans to create splendid floats, decorations, and music. Religious ceremonies adopted a carnival-like atmosphere, which included plays and narrations, and they went to extraordinary lengths to create beautiful offerings to the gods and the spiritual realms. Many Javanese and even Muslim states of western Southeast Asia later claimed to be related or at least linked to the mighty Majapahit Empire of the 14th and 15th centuries. However, it is Bali that can claim more than a historical recognition of the suzerainty of the Majapahits since their people are, in fact, the true heirs to the historical kingdom.

Along with the architectural and religious heritage brought from eastern Java, the Kawi script (the ancestral forerunner of the Javanese and Balinese written language common to Southeast Asia at the time), painting, sculpture, and the Wayang (Wayang Kulit or Wajang) puppet theater also lay claim to having their origins in Majapahit. The Wayang puppet shows are a particularly unique and fascinating piece of local culture and are recognized by the United Nations UNESCO as a vital part of Indonesia's ancient heritage. The Wayang puppets are either three-dimensional dolls or two-dimensional leather (or wood) shadow puppets with stylized features and clothing. The dramatic shows are watched behind lit screens and communicate indigenous knowledge, mythology, and folklore or important philosophies, such as those found in the two quintessential ancient Hindu epic poems—the *Ramayana* and the *Mahabharata*. These two pieces of ancient Hindu literature are dated between the 7th century BCE and the 4th century CE and are considered some of the main scriptural references of the religion. Over time, the tradition of Wayang has grown to include live action, singing, dancing, music, literature, painting, and other symbolic art forms. Although, interestingly, the Bali Aga were never brought into the cultural renaissance of the Majapahit era.

When the influx of Majapahit influences began in the 14th century with the overthrow of the Balinese royalty, eastern Javanese-style royal courts were established in Bali by royalty and priests alike.

Intermarriages of prominent (or royal) Balinese families with Majapahit royalty began formulating the upper-class caste of future Balinese societies. Besides the family lineages, cultural and religious descendancies began to become entrenched as island ideologies, cultural norms, and art forms. The indigenous spoken language developed to incorporate elements of Javanese. Most importantly, a wealth of ancient Buddhist-Hindu literature, such as the *Nagarakretagama*, was maintained in the royal libraries of Bali and neighboring Lombok (also part of the Majapahit Empire). The palm-leaf eulogy poem *Nagarakretagama*, written in the 14th century by a Buddhist monk, tells the story of the ancient Hindu-Buddhist kingdoms and specifically speaks of the Majapahit Empire and its most influential leader, Hayam Wuruk. Hayam Wuruk ascended the throne in the same era that chief minister (*patih*) Gajah Mada, who'd led the attack on Bali, was at the pinnacle of his career. It is likely that Gajah Mada was a significantly influential person in guiding Hayam Wuruk's eventual domination throughout much of the Indonesian archipelago. After the end of Hayam Wuruk's reign, the Majapahit Empire began to decline as a power base, but its influence as a political and cultural phenomenon was transferred, mostly to Bali, and the island remains an icon of Hindu-Buddhist Javanese culture and fiefdom to this day.

The Majapahit period in history is marked by the extensive Indianization of Southeast Asia, and it was the most influential foreign power in the establishment of the socio-cultural historical landscape of Bali. The Majapahit influence reached as far afield as the Malay Peninsula and eastern Indonesia. The era bequeathed Bali with the most lasting influences of its present-day social structure and class system, as well as architecture, temples, and the royal hierarchy. The Majapahit migration had given rise to significant advancements in culture, arts, and the economy, eventually birthing a Balinese national identity consisting of several Hindu kingdoms. The geographical extent of these Hindu kingdoms is echoed in Bali's existing eight governing regencies (or *kabupaten*)—their extent has not changed much since their formation several hundred years ago.

The historical link between the Majapahit Empire and the resident rulers of Bali became intertwined from the time that Gajah Mada (the Javanese prime minister) led a successful attack on the Balinese king in Bedulu (near Ubud) in 1342, which culminated in 1343. Gajah Mada's general, Arya Damar, assisted in the overthrow of Bali, which was achieved after a series of battles that took place over the course of seven months. The Majapahit governance of Bali was handed over to Arya Damar's four younger brothers. The leading brother, Arya Kenceng, went on to become the ancestor of the Balinese kings of the Tabanan and Badung royal houses. According to the Balinese babad, the Majapahit capital was located at Samprangan (or Samplangan, Gianyar) and then later at Gelgel (southeastern coast beyond Gianyar). The babad, chronicles, or dynastic genealogies were a large and scattered set of mostly 19th-century Brahmin-authored texts of Balinese history, dating back to the start of the Majapahit era, although it is considered to be a mix of fact, legend, and indigenous myth. Specifically, a 20th-century babad known as the *Babad Buleleng* was scribed at a time (1920) when Bali's Dutch colonizers were seeking to reinstate the nation's traditional kingdoms and rulers. This babad was thought to have been contrived in support of the appointment of I Gusti Putu Jelantik as ruler of the Buleleng Regency. The *Babad Buleleng* could be an example of a summary of all of the babad that came in the centuries before, although nothing can be confirmed.

Three earlier texts, *Babad Dalem*, *Usana Bali*, and *Usana Jawi*, establish (at least in cultural terms) the lineage of certain Balinese royal families, tracing their origins back to the original Majapahit conquerors. These earlier texts (and sometimes poetic verses) appear to have been written at the start of the 18th century, following a time when Balinese political power was shifting from the dominant Gelgel to the emerging Klungkung dynasty (c. 1687). Since the babad were often written to ascertain genealogical descendancy for those gaining power, their accuracy is significantly questionable, but they do provide some idea of overarching historical truths or ideas as well as common historical linkages.

The *Babad Dalem* (the *Chronicle of Kings*) is the babad that deals specifically with the history of Gelgel and suggests that the kingdom remained the primary Balinese stronghold until the second half of the 17th century, well after the dissolution of Majapahit. The Gelgel domination gave way to the Klungkung dynasty as the rightful inheritors of the Balinese kingdom, at least according to the babad. Despite contest by other kingdoms of Bali, Klungkung continued to rule in one sense or another for more than two centuries until the final 20th-century conquest by the Dutch in 1908. The ability of Klungkung to retain power came largely from the *Babad Dalem*'s description of the dynasty as having descended directly from the Majapahit Empire! Although many Balinese kingdoms attempted to write and interlink babad that "proved" their ancestral lineage to the Majapahit and their "rightful" place to overrule the other Balinese kingdoms, these efforts were very obviously contrived. The creation of Balinese babad would surge at times when political change threatened to engulf the island, such as in the mid-18th century and during Dutch colonial rule.

According to the *Babad Dalem*, once Majapahit had conquered the king of Bali in the royal center of Bedulu, a vassal court was established in Samprangan, Gianyar, close to the previous royal center. Legendary sources such as the babad are confusing and contradictory, and their timelines are almost impossible to believe, especially when compared to early 16th-century accounts by the first European explorers. What is factually clear is that the Majapahit vassal royal courts of Bali consisted of eastern Javanese noblemen and priests, as well as warriors (Brahmin and Kshatriya), from whom many people on Bali in the modern day can claim descendancy (and not exclusively from the royal houses). Apocryphal evidence indicates that the Majapahit rulers moved to Bali in groups over periods of time after the conquest in 1343 and established vassal courts that provided the foreign support structures required to retain influence over Bali. The Javanese overlords may have set up more than one capital on the island and are likely to have met resistance, particularly from the independent Bali Aga of the mountainous regions. According to legend, one of the first rulers of Samprangan, Sri Aji Kresna Kepakisan, had three sons. The eldest (Dalem Samprangan) was incompetent, and when his younger brother, Dalem Ketut, succeeded to the throne, he moved the royal center to Gelgel (southern Klungkung coast). Samprangan lapsed into obscurity, and the royal center of Gelgel continued for at least a century.

Chapter 5 – Gelgel and the Muslim Era

Gelgel is on the southeastern coast of the Klungkung Regency of Bali. It is believed to have been an ancient seat of power from the early 1500s, coinciding with the fall of the Majapahit Empire as well as the arrival of Islam and early European explorers in Bali. The Gelgel kingdom continued as the dominant indigenous power until the mid- to late 1600s, being replaced by the Dewa Agung of Klungkung. It is likely that Gelgel achieved stability when the Sultanate of Demak fell in the mid-16th century and was replaced by the Javanese Muslim Sultanate of Pajang and later by the Mataram Sultanate—not to be confused with the Mataram (Medang) Kingdom of the 11th century CE. In its time, the *puri* (Balinese court) of Gelgel was a vital center of the island's polity and religion—two aspects of Balinese life that remain indivisible to this day.

Gelgel's link to the previous Majapahit dynasties is only recorded in babad and so cannot be verified. Some historians believe that there may be no direct ancestral link between the end of the Majapahit regencies and the more intrinsically "Balinese" court of Gelgel and later Klungkung. The babad, which were written several hundred years later, may have been an afterthought and a direct attempt by the authors to both promote their own bloodlines as those of the upper classes and also entrench Bali as a Hindu state, although the *Babad Dalem* can be backed up by European sources in certain instances. With the encroachment of Islamic forces beginning in the early 16th century, the Balinese became ever-insistent upon their true identity as ancestors of the mighty Hindu Majapahit. An account from the 19th century explains why it was difficult for the Balinese kingdoms to unite as one or even for a single foreign power to overcome the island throughout its history. Helen M. Creese's (an associate professor at the University of Queensland, Australia) *Bali in the Early 19th Century the Ethnographic Accounts of Pierre du Bois* describes the poetic accounts of a Dutch governmental bureaucrat's experiences as a civil administrator in the 1830s in Badung. Pierre du Bois explained how the geography of Bali determined its governance structure since the regions were often divided by deep ravines or high mountains with no navigable rivers and few roads. He explained that the roads were dangerous because of tigers and malefactors—presumably bandits!

The Gelgel region was home to a series of powerful kings, the Raja Dalem of Gelgel, a powerful *patih* (prime minister), and a considerable royal harem. The dominions of Gelgel were known to extend at times beyond Bali itself to include the eastern islands of Lombok and Sumbawa and the far eastern Javanese area of Blambangan. Gelgel was in a continual state of unrest, as relatives of the ruling classes and other Balinese kingdoms continued to disrupt the status quo and contest the right of Gelgel to rule. A VOC (Dutch East India Company) source in 1619 reported no fewer than thirty-three petty kingdoms operating under the Raja Dalem. The Dutch reported on a particularly painful uprising dating to approximately 1585 to 1587 in which the king overcame an attempted coup and ultimately banished the usurpers to a barren island just off Bali. Meanwhile, the Malay Archipelago was becoming increasingly Islamized, and this conversion was encroaching rapidly upon eastern Java, where the Hindu-Buddhist ancestors of the vanquished

Majapahit Empire were considered to be heathens by the surrounding Muslims.

Although Muslim traders had been active in the Malay Archipelago since the 8th century CE, it would take another five hundred years before the spread of Islam began in earnest in Nusantara. Scholastic missionaries from South and Southeast Asia, as well as the Arabian Peninsula, brought the teachings of Islam to Bali's neighboring islands, including Sumatra and Java. The success of the spread of Islam was via its adoption at first by rulers and elites, as well as traders, from where it spread to the population at large. By the end of the 13th century, Islam had been established in northern Sumatra, which was noted by the European explorer Marco Polo (1254–1324 CE). Evidence of a Muslim sultanate and ruling dynasty dates from this time.

The spread of Islam was slow at first, but it gained momentum at certain times, such as during the 15th century with the Malacca Sultanate. The small but powerful regional historical capital of the Malay Peninsula, Malacca, was strategically positioned adjacent to a sea strait separating the mainland from Sumatra. The Malacca Strait was the main entry channel into Nusantara and the region of Malacca, and the Islamic sultanate that grew around it, the Malacca Sultanate, became central to the rise and fall of powerful influences across the Malay Archipelago. Of course, the spread and impact of Islam were heavily dependent upon the maritime trade routes. Sea traders spread the word of Islam and carried scholars and goods associated with the newly Islamized regions. The Malacca Sultanate's strategic position on the Malaysian trade routes gave it the military power to accelerate the spread of Islam. The decline of the Majapahit kingdom that had dominated trade until the early 1500s coincided with the rise of several powerful sultanates that had developed across Nusantara, including the Demak Sultanate of central Java. The Chinese joined the maritime trade race and created Chinese Islamic communities throughout the islands. An Islamized trade hegemony developed across maritime Southeast Asia, which was protected by mainland China and other Islamic states to the north.

By the end of the 16th century, Islam dominated Sumatra and Java. It should be noted that the conversion to Islam was not generally accompanied by bloodshed in the early centuries. Sufism (Muslim mysticism) was considered the vehicle whereby Muslims incorporated local elements of animism, Hinduism, and Buddhism into the Islamic faith, eventually converting believers by making established and local belief systems part of Islam. From the 17th century onward, more traditional Islamic influences began arriving from the Arabian Peninsula (rather than Asia), and they brought with them a more orthodox and forceful version of the religion. When the Dutch gained interest in the trade benefits of Nusantara in the early 17th century, they enabled the spread of Islam by displacing established Muslim traders, who then relocated to smaller ports throughout the archipelago.

A buffer empire between Bali and the fully converted western and central Javanese Muslim states still existed: the area of Blambangan. Blambangan, located in the far eastern corner of Java, was the last remaining stronghold of the vanquished Majapahit Empire. As the main inheritors of the Majapahit culture, Bali and Blambangan relied on each other for trade but also as the last remaining vestiges of a disappearing culture. At the same time, Balinese royal infighting forced the Raja Dalem to look outside the bounds of Bali for support. In 1639, the Sultanate of Mataram (the adjacent Islamic Javanese state to Blambangan) launched an invasion on Blambangan in order to spread the Islamic faith to all of Java. Gelgel supported its neighbor in rebuffing the Mataram troops, although Blambangan was ultimately forced to surrender. Luckily, however, once the Mataram troops had withdrawn, the death of the sultan of Mataram forced them to look inward, and they lost interest and momentum in pursuing an overthrow of Blambangan and Bali.

Both Blambangan and Bali had survived the full collapse of Majapahit in 1527, and Blambangan remained stubbornly "heathen" (Hindu-Buddhist) until the second half of the 18th century—250 years later. Bali's ability to remain outside of the Muslim fray until modern times is truly remarkable. The island's outlying location within the Indonesian arc of islands probably had the biggest role to play in Bali's ability to retain its identity, religion, and ethnicity. Aside from geography, Blambangan—as part of far eastern Java and Bali's closest connection to the rest of Nusantara—can be attributed as one of the factors that prevented Bali from being swept up in the tide of Islamic conversion in later centuries. Blambangan was the last remaining non-Islamic stronghold that extended from the Malay Peninsula, across Sumatra, and down through Java. This Hindu-Buddhist outpost protected Bali geo-politically from direct and overwhelming Islamic conversion. Blambangan spent so much time squabbling with its neighboring Muslim sultanates that Bali was perhaps both geographically and politically more removed from the Islamic states than would have been the case otherwise (such as if the whole of Java had become Muslim in the early 1500s.) As an example, the oldest mosque in Bali, the Masjid Nurul Huda Gelgel, in Gelgel was built in the late 16th century by Muslim missionaries from Java who refused to go home after failing to make converts! Evidence suggests that historically, the Islamic conversions that did occur in Bali happened gradually and peacefully.

Meanwhile, the indomitable rulers of Gelgel embarked on a series of unsuccessful wars with the eastern Javanese Islamic regional powers of Pasuruan and Mataram, which lay directly to the west of Blambangan. Both the Balinese babad and European sources (such as the Dutch register of the VOC, the Dagh-Register) reported both failed and successful skirmishes with Mataram, of which Gelgel was a part. (However, historical records mostly suggest that Bali's attempts to invade eastern Islamic Java were embarrassing and abortive.) Apocryphal evidence describes the leaders of Gelgel as despising Islam, although early European explorers noted that Bali traded peacefully with Muslims from across the archipelago. In about 1630, an envoy of the VOC (Dutch East India Company) was posted to Bali to create a treaty against the Javanese Muslim state of Mataram. However, the envoy (Van Oosterwijck) was met with refusal by the Gelgel king, who wished to remain on peaceful terms with both the Muslim sultanates and the Dutch. This contradiction in the Gelgel kingdom's handling of foreign Muslim powers may reflect the attitudes and behaviors of changing generations, which is supported in the babad.

By the mid-1500s, the successor of Dalem Ketut (the first Gelgel ruler), Dalem Baturenggong, was enthroned, and his reign marked the pinnacle of the Gelgel kingdom—the golden age of the Balinese Gelgel. Baturenggong's era extended until after the middle of the 16th century, after which his two sons, Bekung and Saganing (Seganing), reigned until the first quarter of the 17th century. Dalem Bekung was said to have ruled during a troubled time in which two rebellions, in 1558 and 1578, by his courtiers, as well as a severe military defeat against the Islamic Javanese kingdom of Pasuruan, threatened to destabilize his rule. His brother, Dalem Saganing, apparently enjoyed a long and peaceful rule. During Baturenggong's (Dalem Bekung's and Dalem Saganing's father) apogee, Bali, Lombok, and parts of easternmost Java were united under his suzerainty. However, the ownership of Lombok was contested, with the Makassar kingdom of south Sulawesi claiming it as well.

Justus Heurnius, a Dutch chaplain of Batavia—or Jakarta—assisted in translating the Bible into Indonesian languages. In his 1638 report, he describes a very close relationship between the kings of Gelgel and their priests or Brahmana. Dalem Baturenggong became the patron of a priest, or a Brahmin sage, named Nirartha, who had escaped the Islamic Javanese island and sought refuge in Bali. Ironically, along with advancing Islam, in around 1540, Bali experienced a Hindu renaissance led by Nirartha. As a Hindu-Buddhist high-priest, Nirartha was at the center of the spiritual and cultural revolution that occurred in Bali after the final collapse of Majapahit. Nirartha was intent upon spreading the concept of dharma ("righteousness") throughout Bali.

Dang Hyang Nirartha (Dang Hyang Nirarta Rauh or Pedanda Shakti Wawu Rauh), also known as "the Brahmin of Brahmins," was responsible for creating numerous literary works that formed the basis of Balinese Hinduism. These texts consisted mostly of high-quality hymns or kakawin. Kakawin are long narrative verses of ancient Javanese and Balinese origin. The verses are derived from Sanskrit literature in the style of ancient Hindu mythological and religious texts. The kakawin were most actively in circulation from the 9th to the 16th centuries and were brought to life in plays and recitals. The poems are rich sources of information on court life of the time, as well as spiritual ideologies threaded through intricate fables.

Nirartha was not only an advocate of religious texts and literature but was also an adherent of temple-building. Legends suggest that Nirartha was one of the first Hindu-Buddhists to arrive from Java after 1527 and that, while waiting for his family, he built the Perancak Temple. Perancak Temple in Jembrana—on the western side of Bali— stands to commemorate Nirartha's arrival on the island in circa 1537 from the Javanese royal court of Blambangan. Under his direction, Nirartha was responsible for erecting thirty-four temples throughout Bali, including several sea temples (Pura Segara). Nirartha oversaw the erection of a string of sea temples along the southwest coast of Bali, with each one being visible from the next. He was said to have done this to honor the sea gods and provide a chain of spiritual protection for the island.

In some instances, it is possible that Nirartha may not have been directly responsible for building all of the temples that were later attributed to him by the Balinese. He may have been more instrumental in bringing people's attention back to them and their prerequisite holiness. Essentially, Nirartha was a teacher and an advocate of spirituality within everyday life. He encouraged and prescribed the designs for the Balinese village temples, which are still an important element of life today. The Suranadi Temple in Lombok was apparently the work of Nirartha, and since Bali's closest island neighbor to the east was under the control of Gelgel during this time, it also became home to certain religious texts and babad. (Most of these were later removed by the Dutch and their Balinese consorts at the turn of the 20th century during a series of Dutch invasions.)

Amongst Nirartha's other accomplishments was his introduction of the padmasana (lotus throne) shrine in honor of the supreme god, Acintya. The padmasana formed the basis for Shiva worship later in Bali, which adopted a similar image. As a result, Nirartha is often ascribed as being a priest of Shaivite Hinduism. The padmasana temple architecture, as derived from the Javanese architecture of the same type, has become emblematic of Balinese religious structures. Nirartha's contribution to Bali's reputation as the "Island of the Gods" is noteworthy. He was also known as Wawu Rawuh ("coming together") in his close association with the king and by his appointment as a bhagawanta (royal priest). Nirartha enjoyed a prestigious religious lineage and was descended from renowned Javanese holy men. In particular, his grandfather, Mpu or Dang Hyang Tantular Angsokanatha, was the author of the critical Hindu-Buddhist work the *Kakawin Sutasoma*. The *Kakawin Sutasoma* is an ancient Javanese poem (c. 14th century CE) and the source of the Indonesian motto "Unity in Diversity." The poem teaches religious tolerance, particularly between Hindu and Buddhist religions.

Indigenous texts tell of Nirartha's psychic abilities and his prediction of the end of Javanese Hindu-Buddhist culture. The advent of a series of natural disasters around the end of the Majapahit Empire reinforced the priest's belief that their god did not intend the dharmic way to continue in Java, and this precipitated his move to Bali. Along with the reinvigoration that Nirartha brought to Balinese Hindu-Buddhism and the spread of dharma (right living) was the concept of *moksha*—a state of enlightenment that eliminated the need for rebirth. Nirartha is attributed with founding the Balinese Shaivite priesthood to which all Balinese priests (*pedandas*) of today can claim association. Legends say that he used his psychic abilities to select the correct locations for temples.

Although not attributed to Nirartha, Bali's "mother temple" is the Hindu Besakih Temple (Pura Besakih) on the slopes of the mystical volcano Gunung Agung (twenty-seven kilometers or seventeen miles north of Gelgel). Built almost one thousand meters above sea level, the temple complex has eighty-six separate but interlinked clan temples and shrines spread over six levels. It is considered Bali's largest and most important temple. The origins of Besakih date from the 8th century when a Hindu monk created a housing complex at the area called "Basuki," named after the dragon deity Naga Besukian believed to inhabit Mount Agung (from where the name evolved to Besakih). The complex was in use as a place of worship by the 13th century, and by the 15th century, it was the main temple used by the Gelgel kingdom. The temple has been added to over time and has fortunately escaped any damage by eruptions from Mount Agung. Locals claim this to be a sign from the gods. Like all Balinese temples, Besakih is an open-air compound of many separate walled areas joined by interleading gates. A series of stairways, terraces, pavilions (*bale*), courtyards, and shrines (*candi*) lead the worshiper up toward the sacred mountaintop and culminate in an inner temple and the padmasana, which was completed in the 17th century. Typical of Balinese temples, Besakih is punctuated with bamboo banners (long adorned poles), pagodas, sacred cloths, colorful plants, and offerings from worshipers.

Pura Besakih, Karangasem, Bali, showing the Javanese style split gateway entrance with Mount Agung behind

Pura Besakih, Karangasem, Bali, with Meru (multi-tiered tower) shrines.

As a royal consort during the golden age of Gelgel, Nirartha was most influential in contributing to the complexities of Balinese religion and the creation of a unique form of Hinduism and, subsequently, the idiomatic nature of Balinese culture. This uniqueness in culture and religion was one factor that enabled Bali to withstand the sweeping influences of Islam across Nusantara allow the population to resist mass conversion. More than 80 percent of modern-day Bali's population are practicing Hindus, and approximately 12 percent are adherents of Islam. Bali remains the only non-Muslim majority province of Indonesia. However, despite the Balinese *Babad Dalem* claiming that the Balinese Gelgel remained firmly in control of Bali, several historical sources suggest that Bali was more officially under Muslim rule, specifically in the second half of the 16th century. Bali's ability to resist complete Islamic domination is probably due to a combination of factors. The geopolitical buffer zone of Blambangan, Bali's unique geographical position, its historical resistance to excessive trade relations, and its individualized Hinduism and culture meant Bali was more impervious to total Islamic conversion than the rest of Nusantara.

In approximately the first half of the 17th century, Lombok was a part of Bali and possibly Sumbawa as well. Early European records suggest that Bali was a largely rural society, well populated and agriculturally successful, one over which the ruling classes enjoyed high (but perhaps remote) prestige. Gelgel may have flourished during this period in accordance with the Indonesian "age of commerce"—a time when Southeast Asian maritime trade was booming. Although Bali's formal role in trade during this period is questionable, there is no doubt that it was part of the Southeast Asian trade networks, specifically via Java. The Balinese exchanged cotton cloth manufactured on the island as well as spices. (The cotton industry came to Bali from India, via Java, in approximately 200 BCE.) In 1620, the Dutch made an abortive attempt to establish closer trade links with the Balinese. They reported that the king was headstrong, and the trade relationship was not established. The Dutch made detailed historical records at the end of the 16th century. Since they failed in their attempts to establish a formal commercial connection with the island, reports on Bali for the next few centuries were largely from diplomats and missionaries.

In the 1630s, the last documented king of Gelgel, Dalem Di Made, ruled tentatively until 1648, when his reign mysteriously ended. By this stage, the kings of Gelgel ruled in close association with two contesting families, the Agung and Ler lineages. Also, always closely intertwined with Balinese rulership was a hereditary line of Brahmana preceptors, as well as ministers introduced from various lineages. From 1651, the Gelgel kingdom began to break apart due to internal conflicts to the extent that multiple Dutch sources report a Balinese civil war occurring during this time. By 1686, a new royal center had been established in Klungkung, four kilometers (2.5 miles) north of Gelgel (modern-day Semarapura).

The interim period of more than three decades was punctuated by extreme dynastic infighting. Usurpers of the throne usually had some form of claim, such as ancestral lineage or as younger and overlooked sons of the king. When legitimate protests were ignored, stronger clans were not averse to simply grabbing the throne. One of these usurpers was the minister named Anglurah Agung (Gusti Agung Di Made or Gusti Agung Maruti), who is recorded as having ruled from 1665 to 1686. He is remembered as having briefly had interactions with the Dutch from around 1665 to 1667 and also helping to defend the island of Lombok before he took power in 1665. This was also the era when minor regencies, such as Buleleng, began to assert themselves, and Anglurah Agung struggled to retain power. In 1686, Anglurah Agung fell in battle against noblemen who were loyal to a more formal lineage of Gelgel, including aristocrats from the kingdoms of Buleleng and Badung. The babad tell of the rise of I Dewa (Agung) Jambe (r. c. 1686–1722) in Klungkung in 1683. He was a scion of the old Gelgel line, and Dutch sources corroborate his installment as the new king in 1686, three years after his emergence as a contender to the throne. The capital was moved four kilometers north, and a new Balinese royal rulership began that marked the end of the Gelgel period. (Technically, though, the new rulership retained the Gelgel bloodline.)

The new rulers of Bali, the Dewa Agung (Dewa Agung, or "Great God"), managed to retain some form of domination until the mid-19th century and the arrival of the Dutch colonists. However, the end of the Gelgel kingdom also marked the end of a single Balinese monarchy. The Dewa Agungs were really only responsible for a small area around the Klungkung Palace, as well as the lesser Balinese island of Nusa Penida. Under the Dewa Agungs (who were of the upper religious or Kshatriya caste), the island of Bali was split into nine minor kingdoms: Klungkung, Buleleng, Karangasem, Mengwi (just north of Denpasar), Badung, Tabanan, Gianyar, Bangli, and Jembrana. Each of these nine kingdoms built their own palaces (*puri*), established their own local government, and eventually built their own dynasties. The principality of Mengwi claimed descent from Anglurah Agung.

The smaller local kingdoms of Bali developed their own rulerships and systems over the centuries, but they still pledged allegiance to the Dewa Agung of Klungkung as their primary overlord. Part of their power lay in their possession of ancient Balinese heirlooms (*pusaka*), which were believed to have magical powers that may have originated from Majapahit. (These *pusaka* were rumored to have been handed down from royal generation to generation and sometimes between lineages. Examples include kris or keris—ceremonial daggers—babad, and patterned cloths, like the Indonesian *Songket*.) The Klungkung dynasty remained, at least in nominal terms, as the kings of Bali. These original nine kingdoms of Bali developed into the eight modern-day regencies (*kabupaten*) of Bali (plus the urban node of Denpasar), though the country is run as a province of Indonesia. Before the arrival of the Dutch in the mid-19th century, the Balinese kingdoms fought amongst themselves. By the era of European intervention and colonization, the ruling arrangement on the island was complicated and fragmented. The Dutch used this incoherent Balinese regnal system to their advantage when they sought to take command of the island.

Chapter 6 – Early European Exploration

European influence in the Malay Archipelago was originally orientated around the region of Malacca on the Malay Peninsula. On the southwestern handle of the peninsula, Malacca was a small but strategic node adjacent to the Malacca Strait, which separates the mainland from Sumatra. The Muslim Sultanate of Malacca had been the dominant regional power for about a hundred years, and it was eventually subdued in 1511 by a combination of European forces, specifically the Portuguese and the Dutch. With the advent of modern shipbuilding and the era of oceanic exploration, the Europeans were intent upon controlling the trade routes of the Maritime Silk Road. The Portuguese remained in control of Malacca for a further 130 years until the Dutch overtook all other regional powers. For the first half of the 17th century, the Dutch and Portuguese fought against one another in what was known as the Spice War, as the ultimate aim for all parties was to control the spice trade of the Moluccas (the Maluku Spice Islands in eastern Indonesia). Essentially, the tension on mainland Europe, as well as the newly formed Dutch East India Company, pitted Dutch armadas against the Portuguese across their contested colonies worldwide. In the East Indies, the Dutch were ultimately victorious and remained the dominant power in the archipelagic waters until well into the 20th century.

However, before the advent of the Spice War, European explorers within Nusantara were rare, and their presence in Bali even more unusual. The era of the Italian merchant and explorer Marco Polo (1254-1324 CE) would have brought back indirect news of Bali to Europe since he explored the Indies in the late 13th century and wrote of his experiences whilst spending time on Sumatra and describing life there (there were no specific references to Bali). Historically, the consensus is that the first significant wave of European explorers to Indonesia involved the Portuguese, who were in search of spices and other goods for trade. The Portuguese explorer Vasco da Gama (c. 1460-1524 CE) led the first European ships around the Cape of Good Hope (southern tip of Africa) in 1498, and he was the first European to reach India by sea. Da Gama's expedition provided the maritime knowledge to open the sea routes from Europe to Asia for trade, and so began the Portuguese interventions into Southeast Asia. By 1511, the Portuguese had possession of the port and the greater strategic area of Malacca. The Portuguese colonialist-appointed governor of India at that time, Afonso de Albuquerque, had taken Malacca by force, overcoming the local sultanate in order to control the spice trade that operated primarily through the Malacca Strait.

In 1512, the first official European contact was made with Bali when the Portuguese sent a ship from Malacca to Bali. The expedition was led by António Abreu and Francisco Serrão, and they reached the northern coast of Bali. This was the first expedition of a series of biannual trips that the Portuguese took to the Spice Islands during the century, whereby they skirted the Sunda Islands on their way. In the initial trip of 1512, Francisco Rodrigues mapped Bali. Further interactions, or at least sightings of the island, occurred over the next decades. Bali was referred to as *Boly, Bale,* and *Bally* in early Spanish and Portuguese navigational maps. In 1580, Sir Francis

Drake, sent by the government of Queen Elizabeth I of England, briefly visited the island in search of spices.

There was a failed attempt in 1585 by the Portuguese to establish a fort and a trading post on Bali. The ship that was sent was wrecked on a reef off the Bukit Peninsula. Five survivors made it to shore and apparently joined the Gelgel kingdom! They were provided with homes and wives. Twelve years later, in 1597, the Dutch explorer Cornelis de Houtman arrived in Bali with a greatly diminished crew (probably due to disease). They visited Jembrana, Kuta (Denpasar Peninsula), and finally assembled at Padang Bai (a southeast island, east of Gelgel), where they named Bali *Jonck Holland* (Young Holland). Upon meeting with the king, or Dalem, they became acquainted with one of the sailors from the 1585 wreck, Pedro de Noronha.

In 1601, the second official Dutch expedition of the 17th century was sent to Bali under Jacob van Heemskerck. The Balinese royalty took this opportunity to exchange friendly letters to trade with Prince Maurits, the leader of the Dutch Republic in Europe from 1585 to 1625. This open invitation by Bali for the Dutch to trade freely with their kingdom was misinterpreted and later used by the Dutch to claim overlordship of Bali. The openly friendly and welcoming style of the letter, as well as the obvious naivete of the Balinese Dalem in his statement of, "I grant permission for all who You send me to trade as freely as my own people may [trade] when they visit Holland and for Bali and Holland to be one," is a tragic example of colonial-era misrepresentation.

In 1597, a book was published in Europe in several languages entitled *Verhael vande Reyse by de Hollandsche Schepen gedaen naer Oost Indien* (*Description of a Voyage Made by Certain Ships of Holland into the East Indies*). The book was based on the private journals of an anonymous crew member on board the vessel *Hollandia* (of the VOC or Dutch East India Company) but was published under the name of Captain Cornelis de Houtman. The book included illustrations and descriptions of Balinese practices at the time, such as the Dalem being pulled on a chariot by two white oxen. The beasts were as ornately adorned as the chariot! In the image, the king is surrounded by his armed guards, and they are all naked to the waist, including the king. Another image describes the practice of *sati* (or *suttee*), the ritual sacrifice of a widow by fire after her husband's death. In the illustration, the corpse burns contentedly in a fire pit to which a happy-looking consort feeds fuel to the flames. The wife jumps unafraid into the pit while the local gamelan (indigenous Balinese orchestra) plays on.

In the meantime (until the mid-1600s), Bali experienced very little European interaction for trade or otherwise. Maritime traders of the time mostly sought goods that Bali did not provide, such as spices, silks, minerals, and metals. (Bali was mostly an agricultural rice economy.) The Spice trade, specifically, despite its ubiquity throughout recorded history, was focused primarily on the small island grouping of the Maluku Islands (Moluccas), east of Sulawesi in eastern Indonesia. The European traders were intent upon acquiring the nutmeg, mace, and cloves indigenous to the Maluku Islands, although the trading capital for these was eastern Java, 1,600 kilometers (995 miles) west of the Moluccas. The crops that were so coveted by the world came from just two types of trees on two small clusters of islands in the Moluccas. Cloves (the unopened flowers of the clove trees) were found on five islands, and nutmeg and mace came from the seed and kernel of a single species of tree found on ten islands (the Banda Islands).

In the 16th century, once the Portuguese had control of Malacca, they turned their attention to the Spice Islands. They dominated the regional trade of spices and other goods until the rise of the Dutch East India Company (Dutch: *Vereenigde Oostindische Compagnie* or VOC) in the early 17th century. The VOC was a public-private Dutch mega-consortium focused on maritime trade, and it was founded in the early 17th century. The VOC lasted for two hundred years from its foundation in 1602, and it posed considerable competition to other traders and colonizers around the world during its time. By 1603, the Dutch had established the first permanent trading post on west Java at Bantam (or Banten). The Dutch were intent upon dominating Malacca from the inception of the VOC. In the interim period of a century, starting with the conquest of Malacca in the early 1500s, the Islamic Sultanate of Aceh centered on northern Sumatra had grown into a regional power. The sultanate was not content with the Portuguese controlling the sea corridors of Malacca, and it joined an alliance with the Dutch to take control of Malacca. The alliance finally triumphed in 1641, and Malacca became a Dutch stronghold, with the Portuguese forced out as interlopers into the archipelago. The Dutch moved their headquarters to the Javanese capital of Jakarta, then called Batavia (or Batauia), which had been founded in 1619 by the Dutch. (Batavia was founded on the site of the ruins of Jayakarta, formerly of the Banten Sultanate of northern Java whose center was Banten, known as Bantam to colonialists.) Soon after the Dutch conquest of Malacca, the Portuguese ports of the Spice Islands also fell under the control of the VOC. Numerous European East Indies trading companies were started during this period, and East Indies colonies of European countries were also formed. Portugal was Holland's main rival until the mid-1600s when England (and then Britain) competed with the Dutch for dominance. There were brief interludes by the French into the territory, and the Spanish held an East Indies colony across the Philippines (1565–1898) and other islands, including some of Sulawesi (known historically as Celebes) and the Moluccas (1580–1663).

From the mid-17th century, the Dutch dominated the Malay Archipelago. However, despite the material prosperity and prominent royal rule, the Balinese Gelgel kingdom's dealings with Dutch and Portuguese traders were incidental. Dutch records of the time indicate that the Balinese leadership was reluctant to enter into formal trade negotiations and could be "difficult." The all-powerful VOC were most interested in dominating the archipelagic regions of the

Moluccas, Java, and Sumatra. They took less interest in Bali but tried to open a trading post in 1620 that was unsuccessful because of local hostilities. The mission for the trading post was given to First Merchant Hans van Meldert. He was instructed to purchase "beasts, rice, provisions, and women." He was reported to have returned with only fourteen female slaves and nothing else because trade negotiations had been unsuccessful. Other records of Dutch-Balinese relations in the mid-17th century are sketchy. In 1647 or 1648, a Gelgel king of Bali entered into diplomatic relations with the VOC, and in early 1648, a Dutch gift-giving mission left Batavia for Bali. The Dutch may have foundered on the reefs and never reached Bali, as the crew ended their journey on the neighboring island of Lombok.

During this earlier European era, Bali was mostly visited by private traders dealing in slaves and opium since the Dutch government had given the VOC the monopoly on the spice trade. These traders were primarily from China, Arabia, and other parts of maritime Southeast Asia (although some of these traders did include Dutch privateers). In its time, the VOC had free reign of any waters it traversed, as well as permission by its government to infiltrate and dominate any native culture it came across. The company ran its own financial system and minted its own coins; it conducted its own quasi-judicial system, including imprisonment and executions; it had permission to establish treaties or wage war; and it met with little opposition in colonizing new nations where it was strategically opportune to do so. Southeast Asia was no exception. The bounty of Nusantara's Spice Islands was apparently the cause of the formation of the VOC when a ship laden with profitable exotic spices arrived in Holland in 1596. The Dutch saw the opportunity to detach themselves from the dominant European superpowers of the time—specifically Spain—and form their own independent capitalist entity that could simultaneously carry out state objectives abroad. The VOC was both an international war machine for the Dutch as well as the main source for their treasury.

At the same time as the formation of the VOC, the establishment of the British East India Company was indicative of a worldwide periodical scramble for dominance of the maritime trade routes, which lasted well into the 1800s. (The French East India Company was established in 1664 and lasted for a century.) The British had also set their sights on Southeast Asia, as well as several other locations, and the spice trade. The Europeans had interrupted Arabic dominance of maritime trade in archipelagic Southeast Asia but were also instrumental in siding with the regional sultanates and playing one power off another in strategic attempts to gain control of the region. The European success in dominating the East Indies lay in the subsidence during this era of the sultanates into more fragmented oligarchies. The empire-like sultanates and thalassocracies of the Indian and Muslim kingdoms of Nusantara were disappearing at the same time that European explorers were arriving.

Foreign influences and powerplays within Southeast Asia were largely driven by commercial interests and public-private conglomerates that were actually thinly disguised national war machines. With the eventual collapse of the East India companies in the 1800s (the VOC at the beginning of the century and the British toward the end), foreign interests became "nationalized" interventions within the archipelago, and the introduction of a more formalized style of colonization was established via direct government control. The collapse of the VOC in 1800 marked the rise of the nationalist Dutch East Indies—the Dutch colonial arm of the European Dutch Republic in Southeast Asia, whose headquarters was at Batavia. The Dutch East Indies remained a dominant force in the archipelago until the 20th century except for a brief interim period from 1806 to 1815, known as the French and the British interregnum. The French ruled from 1806 to 1811 and the British from 1811 to 1815. Several factors led to the collapse of the VOC, but the final installment of its ruin was the Fourth Anglo-Dutch War in 1780, which involved worldwide contestation of political power and trading routes, in which the VOC lost half its fleet. Soon after the collapse of the VOC, its ports in

Southeast Asia either became nationalized under the newly formed Dutch Republic or became British.

On the other side of the world, the Napoleonic Wars (1803–1815), led by the French military leader Napoleon Bonaparte following the late 18th-century French Revolution, were devastating Europe. Napoleon sought widespread domination, including of the East Indies. The time period from 1806 to 1811 was when the Dutch operated as a vassal of the French, who controlled their continental dominions back home on the European continent. However, constantly at odds with Britain, the French and Dutch powers lost their hold on the East Indies in 1811 when British forces invaded Java, set on dominating the spice trade and access to the Maluku Islands. Java fell to the British in forty-five days, and it was a relatively easy task since it was defended mainly by paid French mercenaries who had little training or leadership.

In 1811, the British colonial official Sir Stamford Raffles (1781–1826) was employed by the British East India Company as secretary to the governor of Malacca. His governorship lasted until 1815, and it was at this point that Raffles decided to take over the government of Batavia. This was a strategic move by Raffles to prevent the French from usurping the British-dominant East Indies, whose power base was Java. Raffles was a key figure in rediscovering ancient Hindu and Buddhist temples and artifacts across Java, including elements of the Majapahit Empire. As an enthusiast of Javanese history, Raffles published a book titled *History of Java* in 1817. Within his East Indies administration, Raffles kept a small contingent of senior British staff but retained the overall Dutch government and civil service. Unfortunately, despite his love for the island and its history, he used high-handed tactics to overthrow local Javanese kingdoms, which resulted in the looting of their cultural and historical content, which were later seized by Raffles. Sir Raffles also attempted to limit the slave trade due to the changing British policies against slavery.

In 1816, after the end of the Napoleonic Wars and the collapse of French power in Europe, the Dutch reasserted their dominance in the region, taking Batavia back under the terms of the Anglo-Dutch Treaty of 1814. The Dutch were intent upon bringing in Europeans to settle the region as a colony to be governed by the Dutch. They were not successful in extending their influence across the archipelago and even caused antagonism on the islands of Sumatra and Java. However, the reestablishment of the Dutch East Indies lasted for another century and brought the wealth and political successes the Dutch had hungered for since the 1500s.

It is said that de Houtman of the late 16th century was fascinated by Bali and the easy charms of its landscape and people. It apparently took him a few months (some records say two years!) to round up his crew to leave. Most European explorers and navigators were motivated primarily by money and material gain, as well as the political control that ensured material gain. Historically, Bali's saving grace was that it didn't offer much in the way of economic gain, and its beauty was not enough to compete with the lure of the bounty of the Spice Islands (Moluccas). So, while the Dutch did not take control of Bali from the 16th to the 18th centuries, they instead established trading posts and used the island as a stopover. Unfortunately, by the mid-19th century, all that changed, and the peaceful island of Bali once again lost its independence.

Chapter 7 – Bali and Colonial Influences

The historical term East Indies broadly included the sum total of islands that stretch for more than 6,000 kilometers (3,728 miles) east of the Indian subcontinent, north of Australia, and south of the Asian mainland. Typically, this included the modern-day Republic of Indonesia (formerly the Dutch East Indies), the Malay Archipelago (including the Philippines), and all other islands of archipelagic Southeast Asia. In its broadest sense, the East Indies sometimes included mainland Southeast Asia as well as the Indian subcontinent, but generally, what colonial traders referred to as the Indies was maritime Southeast Asia.

During its two-hundred-year dominance of the East Indies, the VOC used its strong position in the archipelago to attain slaves to serve in its growing Cape Colony in South Africa, although they mostly took slaves from the Malay Peninsula and parts of East Africa. Within the Southeast Asian archipelago itself, the Dutch used slaves from the region and, in many instances, people who had been enslaved themselves within their own homelands. Bali was in no way immune to the slave trade, and Balinese slaves were brought to Batavia under the VOC's dominion. The Dutch desire for slaves in the centuries of their domination was insatiable since they needed a workforce to settle their colonies across the world, particularly at the African Cape of Good Hope and in the East Indies. During the 18th century, over two-thirds of Batavia consisted of slaves working for the VOC, but by 1853, slavery in the region had technically been abolished due to international pressures. (The official date for the abolition of East Indies slavery may have been a little later—closer to 1860—but the practice continued illegally, particularly by privateers, for years to come, albeit at a vastly reduced rate.)

Balinese slaves were highly prized. The men were valued for their manual labor skills and the women for their beauty and gentle artistry. The kings of Bali were not hesitant to sell off orphans and widows, opponents to their government, criminals, and debtors to slave traders! Although the slaves were employed within Bali itself, on Java (specifically Batavia) and across the Dutch colonies, the biggest market for the slave trade was in French Mauritius (a small island in the Indian Ocean). Payment for the Balinese slaves would be made in opium, and the main port for the unhappy dealings in slaves and opium was through a northern exit in Buleleng known as Singaraja (or "Lion King"). Singaraja remained an important port throughout Bali's history, not only for the island but also for the entire Lesser Sunda Islands. The British were eager to get involved in this Balinese trade to the consternation of the Dutch. Dutch-Balinese relations had never been fortified, and during their 450-year-long association with Bali, their interactions swung from unclear to violent and back again. The two sovereignties realized that they needed each other in the changing and competitive times in which they lived, but neither seemed prepared to make the necessary sacrifices or commitment that was required for a long-term association.

The Sultanate of Mataram was the last Muslim stronghold that dominated Java before the final oppression by the Dutch in the mid-18th century under the auspices of the VOC. The independent sultanate had operated from central Java (not to be confused with the

Mataram Kingdom of the 11th century) since the late 1500s. The sultanate reached the peak of its power in the first half of the 17th century during the reign of Sultan Agung Hanyokrokusumo but began to decline after his death in 1645. A century later, by 1749, the Sultanate of Mataram became a vassal state of the Dutch VOC. The Dutch had attempted to make alliances with Bali in their fight against Mataram and sent an envoy, Van Oosterwijck, in 1633 to obtain a treaty with the king of the Gelgel kingdom. The Dutch attempt was futile, but when Mataram invaded Bali six years later in 1639, the Balinese, in turn, sought Dutch help, which did not arrive. The Balinese Dewa Agung managed to repel Mataram alone. Shortly afterward, the Gelgel kingdom disintegrated to give rise to the Klungkung dynasty.

Bali experienced the brief French interlude into the East Indies at the beginning of the 19th century, but like many other interludes into Balinese life, the alliance passed by unmanifested. When the Javanese administration switched to Franco-Dutch in 1806, Napoleon Bonaparte assigned the "Iron Marshal" Willem Daendels as the new governor-general of Batavia. Bonaparte also sent ships and reinforcements to take control of the East Indies and embarked upon a flurry of fort-building along the Javanese coast. The French were most concerned about the British taking control of the East Indies, which they inevitably did from 1811 to 1815. Daendels signed a Franco-Dutch treaty of alliance with the Balinese king of Badung (central-southern region) in 1806. Klungkung is not mentioned in this treaty. The main premise of the treaty was to provide workers and soldiers for the Franco-Dutch fortifications, mostly on Java. Five years later, Java fell to the British, and the Balinese treaty was not implemented in full.

Under the British governor of Java, Sir Stamford Raffles, several unsuccessful attempts were made with Bali to create positive Balinese-British relations. Raffles made himself extremely unpopular with various Balinese kingdoms when he began infringing on the slave trade in the region in alignment with the abolition policy that was beginning at home in Britain. (Slavery remained widespread during Raffles's tenure, and he was served by a large retinue of slaves at his official residence in Java!) He angered the rajas of Buleleng and Karangasem on Bali, who subsequently sent a military mission against the British-Javanese Blambangan in 1814, which fought British sepoys (Indian mercenaries trained and employed by the British East India Company). In the same year, Raffles sent an envoy to Bali to attain an acknowledgment of submission to his overlordship, and the following year, he himself visited the island. But whatever the outcome of these interactions, Bali once again slipped out of the colonial noose, as the Javanese government changed again to Dutch in 1816 at the end of the Napoleonic Wars.

The Dutch had been subservient to French and British colonial powers for a decade during the French and British interregnum, and they took the opportunity from 1816 onward to reassert their dominance in the Indies. A special commissioner, H. A. van der Broek, was sent to Bali to ratify "concept contracts" for overlordship, which the Balinese refused to accept. Despite Bali's disregard for colonialization, Dutch control expanded across the Indonesian archipelago in the early 1800s, including in Bali. Bali's independent kingdoms were already established, but inter-kingdom warfare was common and continuous between the Balinese rajas. They typically did not operate as a single homogenous unit with common ideals, and there was no clear hierarchy for rulership, governance, or even basic laws. The territory was ripe for foreign intervention, and it was really only the Dutch who made a delayed and unsteady grab for the island.

Denmark made a brief foray into Bali's history in the first half of the 1800s through the actions of a sailor named Mads Lange, who lived in Bali from 1839 to 1856. Lange entered Indonesia aboard a Danish commercial ship as a crew member. The ship harbored at Lombok as well as at Bali. Lange took the opportunity to side with the Balinese king during a Balinese-Lombok series of skirmishes that, luckily for him, saw Bali as the victor. Mads Lange was keen to use any rifts in local governance to establish himself as an independent tradesman. He traded anything that was available, from gold and precious stones to spices, fabric, and livestock, and based himself on the southern peninsula of the island in the Kuta region (southwest Denpasar).

Lange had created a revolutionary new style of independent trade (both importing and exporting to third parties) in an environment when nations had previously dominated the trade routes. Along with his increasing wealth came danger, and by the mid-19th century, the Dane—who became known as the "King of Bali"—had eventually built a compound complete with armaments and trained guards. He eventually had three children with Balinese women who integrated into Balinese royalty in time. His only child by a Chinese woman, Cecilia, married into the Indonesian Sultanate of Johor (south of Malacca on the Malay Peninsula), and Lange's grandson through this alliance, Ibrahim, eventually became the sultan of Johor. Lange's descendants rule the Sultanate of Johor to this day.

In 1843, a contract with the Dutch East Indies placed Klungkung (the main regency of Bali) under Dutch suzerainty. Contracts with other Balinese kingdoms were simultaneously constructed, but they were disputed by the Balinese, and controversies arose regarding their interpretation. This controversy led to Dutch intervention, and between 1846 and 1849, many wars were initiated by the Dutch in their attempt to capture and control Bali. As their influence over the East Indies grew, they became determined to be overlords of this unique but rebellious little island. The Dutch unsuccessfully invaded the north of Bali in 1846 and 1848, but by 1849, they had control of Buleleng and Jembrana. The considerable Royal Dutch East Indies Army fleet that arrived in 1849 to achieve this final overthrow of northern Bali consisted of one hundred ships, three thousand sailors, and five thousand trained soldiers, mostly Dutch.

The European overlords used various excuses to explain their desire for ruling Bali. These excuses mostly included a decision to eliminate the slave and opium trade, arms dealing, and the Balinese practice of plundering shipwrecks, or *tawan karang*. With the assistance of some Balinese kings, who used the colonizers to achieve their own ends, the Dutch eventually took control of the north of the island. The kingdoms of Buleleng and Bangli had always been at odds with each other, and Bangli eventually assisted the Dutch in overthrowing both Buleleng and Jembrana, giving the colonizers control of northern Bali. The chief advisor of Buleleng (I Gusti Ketut Jelantik) managed to escape to Karangasem (eastern Bali) with the raja of Buleleng, but they were killed soon after by Lombok soldiers, who were allies of the Dutch brought to Bali to fight. At this point, the raja of Karangasem committed ritual suicide. I Gusti Ketut Jelantik's open hostility and offensive efforts toward the Dutch invasions of the era have made him a national hero. Unfortunately, the remainder of his household tragically participated in the *puputan*, or mass ritual suicide, which included at least four hundred of his followers. The Dutch had lost a handful of men, but the Balinese casualties were very high (possibly in the thousands).

The *puputan* would become a consistent part during the Dutch overthrow of Balinese royal houses from then on, much to the consternation of the Dutch, who preferred either surrender or open warfare. Reports indicate that the Dutch were horrified by the ritual suicides but that they were also unable to stop them. After the conquest of the north, the Dutch were reluctant to march their troops overland and chose to sail to the south (to Padang Bai) to invade Klungkung. However, the Dutch troops were beginning to slow due to tropical diseases, specifically dysentery. When the Balinese launched a nighttime attack on the Dutch, their commander general, A. V. Michiels, was killed by Klungkung warriors, and the Dutch retreated to their ships. The colonizers had been unable to strike a final blow on southern Bali, and they had suffered heavy causalities during the night raid in Kusamba, which was led by Dewa Agung Istri Kanya.

The Dutch were repelled by a force of 33,000 Balinese from Badung, Gianyar, Tabanan, and Klungkung, and from the safety of their ships, the 1849 incursions had reached a stalemate. The standoff led to a peace treaty with the region, in which Klungkung enjoyed autonomous rule under the sovereignty of the Dutch. Holland still did not control the core of Bali despite this half-hearted attempt to gain Klungkung.

During these struggles, which lasted from 1846 to 1849, the Dutch took the opportunity to recruit troops from Lombok that they brought over in their ships to help overthrow Bali. The Dutch alliance with Lombok was not difficult to achieve since Bali had interfered in Lombok's rulership for centuries. Lombok had been part of the larger Majapahit Empire from before the 14th century, although there had been little recorded of the island before the 17th century. Lombok had largely been made up of petty feuding tribes overseen by Sasak princes (the Sasak people compose the majority of Lombok's population today). The Balinese, specifically Karangasem or eastern Bali, had taken advantage of this fragmentation and took control of western Lombok (a populated area known as Mataram) in the early 1600s, which was already a Muslim state. The Dutch had completed their first treaty with Lombok in 1674 via the VOC and the Sasak princes. By 1750, Bali ruled most of Lombok. In the west of the island, the rulership was largely peaceful and homogenous, but in the east of Lombok, the Balinese were mostly considered as overlords and tax collectors, so they needed to defend their position. By 1838, the Mataram Balinese grouping controlled Lombok, and a rich Balinese court culture had developed through this neighboring island. But it was evident that the Lombok Mataram considered themselves to be not entirely under the spell of Bali since they signed a treaty with the Dutch in 1843 and then another in 1849 during the Dutch interventions in Bali. Ultimately, they were rewarded with the overlordship of Karangasem when northern Bali fell to the Dutch.

Mads Lange's strategic and powerful position had earned him a minor government position with the Dutch as harbormaster. The Dutch used his good relationships with the Balinese kings to include him in negotiating treaties with Bali. In 1849, the Dutch ratified themselves as having sovereignty over Bali, with the local royalty retaining a de facto rulership. Lombok gained suzerainty over Karangasem. Lange was part of these proceedings in a role as "peacemaker" representing all parties. It appears that he used his unique position mostly to gain commercially, as he continued to sell arms to the Balinese kings, both in their arguments with the Dutch as well as against one another. The Dutch ruled from Singaraja in the north from 1855. From 1855 until 1908, the traditional Balinese royal houses were systematically dismantled by the Dutch and their members invalidated. Some members of the royalty were sent into exile, with their land being confiscated, but the dualistic approach of Dutch rulership saw ex-Balinese royalty employed as *punggawa* (local administrators—traditionally court officials), from where they ingratiated themselves with their Dutch overlords and sought to be of influence in the governance of their land. A well-known Balinese character who assisted the Dutch was I Gusti Putu Jelantik, the author of the infamous *Babad Buleleng*, a self-authored liturgy on his own ancestral claim to the Balinese throne. Jelantik worked as an advisor and an interpreter to the Dutch during their invasions of northern Bali, and this eventually gave him a position of prominence in the disabled royal households as the Dutch stronghold in Bali increased during the century.

In 1856, Lange prepared to depart Bali and return to Denmark, laden with wealth and local acquisitions. He mysteriously and unexpectedly died shortly before his departure. Most suspected the cause of death was assassination through poisoning—his past double-dealings and business affairs may have incited numerous enemies. This murder was never confirmed, and it is very possible he died of illness. Lange's grave and memorial can still be visited in Kuta to this day, as he never left Bali and was buried near his compound. His trading business, which had been in decline, was sold to Chinese merchants.

After the intervention of 1849, the Dutch proceeded to annex the northern territories of Bali. They nominated a Balinese royal but placed a Dutch prefect in control—Heer van Bloemen Waanders—who arrived in Singaraja in 1855. Waanders put his full force behind European-style reforms in the north and as far afield as the Dutch influence would stretch. The Dutch vaccinated against diseases, sought to ban the practice of *suttee* (ritual burning of widows), intervened in the slave and drug trades, sought to improve the agricultural irrigation systems, supported further agriculture, built roads and buildings, developed Singaraja (that is evident within Bali to this day), and built other infrastructure to improve commerce and interactions across the island. The Dutch raised taxes on commerce and agriculture, specifically on the opium trade. They developed the northern port into a major hub, which was visited by numerous local and European ships annually. They even attempted to Christianize the locals, but this proved to be a complete failure. In the half-century between the start of the Dutch hold on the north of Bali and the turn of the 20th century, the Balinese launched rebellions and minor skirmishes that were all quelled by their overlords. The Dutch may have remained as only partial overlords of the island for a long time, but they would not relinquish what they had attained.

By the late 1800s, differences between the southern kingdoms of Bali were being exploited by the Dutch in order to extend their control. A decade-long War of the Rajas, from 1884 to 1894, provided fuel for Dutch intervention. The Balinese raja of Gianyar was finally used by the rajas of Ubud in a devious stratagem to put their own self-interests above those of Balinese sovereignty, and they convinced the raja of Gianyar to relinquish his rule to the Dutch. In 1894, Lombok, Bali's closest neighbor to the east, rebelled against the last vestiges of Balinese rulership. Rebellions had been rife since 1891 when the Balinese overlord of Lombok had attempted to recruit Lombok troops to capture the whole of Bali. The western Lombok stronghold of Mataram (still under Balinese control) had two warships at their disposal—the *Sri Mataram* and the *Sri Cakra*—and they used these to surround rebellious Sasak villages and beat down the resistance to their rule. The Dutch took the opportunity to invade Lombok and unite with the native Sasak chiefs to fight against the Balinese overlords. The Sasak Lombok princes had sent an invitation to the Dutch to rule their island instead of the Balinese on February 20th, 1894. In June of 1894, the governor-general of the Dutch East Indies, Van der Wijck, ratified a treaty with the Sasak rebels and sent an army to Lombok. The Dutch also prevented the import of weapons and supplies from Singapore by the Balinese rulers.

By July 1894, the Dutch had sent warships from Batavia, including more than 100 officers, 1,300 European soldiers, 1,000 indigenous soldiers, and almost 400 horses. Battles between the Dutch and the Balinese rulers continued throughout 1894, in which the commander of the Dutch garrison, P. P. H. van Ham, was killed in a night raid in Mataram (western Lombok capital), along with five hundred of his contingent. By November, the Dutch had sent reinforcements under the new commander general, J. A. Vetter. Mataram was overcome in this final onslaught. Thousands died in the battles or committed ritual suicide, including Balinese royalty. The Balinese raja capitulated, and Lombok was annexed to the Dutch East Indies in 1895. The Dutch had gained Lombok and Karangasem (eastern Bali), and their hold on most of Bali became tighter (which included Bangli and Gianyar), but the southern kingdoms continued to refuse colonization. The older southern Balinese people preached peace, but overall, the citizens refused to yield to the Dutch, and a group of combative young princes defeated the colonizers in a surprise attack. This infringement made the Dutch even more determined to dominate Bali, specifically the kingdoms of Tabanan, Klungkung, and Badung. At the same time that the colonizers were seeking a cause for an all-out assault on Bali, they still struggled to justify their reason for wanting domination.

By 1906, the Dutch had launched offenses against the southern Balinese kingdoms of Badung and Tabanan, and they had weakened Klungkung. Klungkung had remained the de facto head kingdom of Bali since the fall of Gelgel hundreds of years earlier. Finally, in 1908, the Dutch invaded Klungkung and cited containment of the opium trade as their reason for interfering (the details are explained in the following chapter). This final onslaught by the Dutch saw the end of the Balinese royal houses as they had existed since the days of Majapahit. The Dutch had secured their sovereignty as foreign rulers of the East Indies but at an extremely high moral cost. Bali was officially a Dutch protectorate—an ambition that had been initiated by the Dutch more than three hundred years before. The Dutch remained in control of Lombok until the Japanese occupation during the Second World War in 1942. They kept a light hold on Lombok by aligning with both Balinese and Sasak royalty to retain control with a tiny contingent of Dutch officers. Despite the fact that the Dutch seized a vast amount of royal treasure from Lombok (230 kilograms of gold and gold items, 7,000 kilograms of silver and silverware, and three chests of precious stones and jewelry) in the 1894 campaign, they were still considered by the Sasaks as heroic liberators of their island. Part of this treasure was returned to Indonesia in 1977.

Chapter 8 – Independence and Democracy

In 1904, a Chinese schooner wrecked on a coral reef near Sanur. Traditionally, the Balinese had rights to salvage in a common practice known as *tawan karang,* and they plundered the schooner, the *Sri Kumala.* However, the Dutch made unreasonable demands for compensation, which were refused by the raja of Badung and supported by the regions of Tabanan and Klungkung. The king of Tabanan also enraged the Dutch by reintroducing the practice of burning widows, known as *suttee.* These conflicts gave the Dutch a reason to launch a new attack on the southern ports of Bali in 1906 to assert their sovereignty. The arrival of the full force of the Dutch navy (the Dutch East Indies Army or the Sixth Military Expedition) at Sanur launched the Badung War. The Balinese were defiant in their continued desire not to be an occupied nation. The Dutch navy blockaded the southern ports, but their ultimatums were ignored. They subsequently launched naval and ground assaults and eventually marched on the palace of Badung. The Dutch assaults on various villages en route resulted in the Balinese burning their own palaces and refusing to fight or submit. Typically, the Balinese authorities at these villages committed ritual suicide.

The Badung War saw a massive defeat for the Balinese and was ironically not a war at all. The incidents of that time permanently compromised Holland's reputation as an even-handed and reasonable overlord. When the Dutch marched on the Badung palace (Denpasar), they were met within one hundred paces by the raja, who was carried on a palanquin, and thousands of his supporters. The only weapons carried by the Balinese were kris or keris (ceremonial daggers), and they moved silently and passively. The raja, dressed in white cremation clothing, was then ritually killed by a priest using a kris in a voluntary act of ceremonial suicide known as *puputan*. The remainder of the procession either killed themselves or were killed by priests in an act of mass suicide, a clear statement that they would rather be dead than ruled by the Dutch. The Dutch pleaded with the Balinese to surrender, but the Balinese would not, and the event ended in the deaths of approximately four thousand Balinese men, women, and children. Some accounts state that stray bullets resulted in the Dutch firing on the Balinese, but regardless, the result was that the Balinese were completely overcome. It was the end of the royal house of Badung.

Later that same day, a similar event took place at the palace of Pemecutan (Denpasar), claiming the lives of more Balinese people. The raja of Tabanan, Gusti Ngurah Agung, and his son surrendered but committed suicide two days later in a Dutch prison. Not surprisingly, the last remaining independent regency, Klungkung, brokered a peace deal with the colonists. The people of Klungkung were required to destroy their fortifications, give up all firearms, and renounce their import and export taxes. After the tragedy of the Badung War, the Dutch received overwhelmingly negative global attention for the events that had led to the unfortunate outcome of mass suicides and the extermination of a huge number of peaceful, indigenous peoples. Apparently, the Dutch troops plundered and looted the battle scenes and dead bodies and razed what was left of the palaces to the ground, but this is unconfirmed.

Unfortunately, the Dutch colonizers' transparency and economic motive in trying to gain control of the opium trade led to the breakdown in the peace deal negotiated with Klungkung. The Dutch sent troops to quell riots in 1908 that had erupted in retaliation to their attempts to get the monopoly on the drug trade. Riots erupted in Klungkung and in Gelgel. After quelling the riots (which resulted in about a hundred Balinese deaths) in Gelgel, the Dutch marched to Klungkung, to where the raja had fled. The raja of Klungkung, along with two hundred followers, purportedly bravely fought from his position of safety at the palace but was killed by a single Dutch bullet. The king had been armed only with a kris according to a prophecy that it would overthrow the enemy. His six wives and the remainder of the palace procession committed *puputan*, as had their predecessors in 1906. At least two hundred Balinese died that day (April 28th, 1908), and the palace was burned. With this final tragedy, the Dutch had full possession and control of Bali—albeit at a high and bloody cost.

This final occupation by the Dutch marked the end of the Balinese Majapahit Empire that had dominated Bali for four hundred years. Regrettably, the Dutch domination of Bali held little meaning for the Balinese, and it was more of a political and economic stratagem than a true moral victory. The Balinese continued with their daily and spiritual pursuits as they had done when being ruled by the Hindu kingdoms—it made an inconsequential difference to them whom they were governed by. However, politically, the Dutch hold on Bali was tentative, and by 1929, the colonizers sought to reinstate native chiefdoms, or what was referred to in Dutch as *volkshoofd*, in order to create a type of decentralized local government still under their suzerainty. The old kingdoms were to be reinstated as negara (Indonesian autonomous states), and the Balinese royalty was to be reestablished, which naturally led to an upsurge in the creation of babad, Balinese ancestral chronicles proving royal lineage. The Balinese impotency against the terror that the Dutch had instilled saw them using words rather than violence to achieve their ends of freedom or at least renewed tribal recognition and respect. Several babad created by the Balinese fiefdoms were sent to Dutch officials in a petition for the right to the throne of their particular regencies and also to motivate efforts for the creation of their regencies as independent negara. Some of these babad petitions ended up at the Dutch parliament in Holland and came to the attention of Queen Wilhelmina, the reigning Dutch queen of the time. Twenty years after the Badung War, in 1929, a nephew of the last Klungkung ruler, Dewa Agung Oka Geg, was appointed as a regent by the Dutch. About a decade later, in 1938, his status, as well as seven other Balinese regents, was elevated to raja (*zelfbestuurder*, or self-governor, in Dutch).

In 1912, a German visitor, Gregor Krause, took pictures and videos of topless Balinese women, which promoted a surge in European tourism after the First World War, particularly to the Singaraja area (modern-day Buleleng). This upsurge in international travel after the Great War not only brought increased attention to Bali but also an influx of international artists and intellectuals. Included in this number during the 1930s were anthropologists Margaret Mead (1901–1978) and Gregory Bateson (1904–1980), as well as renowned artists Miguel Covarrubias (1904–1957) and Walter Spies (1895–1942). Margaret Mead, an American cultural anthropologist, was a well-known media figure in the 1960s and 1970s. This controversial academic was a key influencer in the sexual revolution of the 1960s due to her work regarding the attitudes of sex and the South Pacific and Southeast Asia. Mead was a proponent of broadening sexual attitudes. Gregory Bateson was an English anthropologist and social scientist who was married to Margaret Mead. Miguel Covarrubias, a Mexican graphic artist and the discoverer of the Olmec civilization, along with his wife, Rosa (Rose), took several trips to Bali and created the book *Island of Bali*, which was filled with her photography of the island. This book was a significant contributor to the tourist rush to Bali that followed. Walter Spies was a Russian-born German primitivist painter, composer, musicologist, and curator. He lived in

Bali from 1927 until his capture in 1942 during the Second World War. Spies was well acquainted with the other intellectuals and artists of the time. The musicologist Colin McPhee (1900–1964) communicated the image of Bali as "an enchanted land of aesthetes at peace with themselves and nature" in his book, *A House in Bali.* McPhee was a Canadian-born Indonesian composer and the first Westerner to make an ethnomusicological study of Bali. He composed music based on the ethnic sounds of Java and Bali that became world-renowned.

During the 1960s, the airport was renovated and began to facilitate international flights. Also, the first major tourist hotel was built in Sanur (the southeast coast of Denpasar), and it was called the Bali Beach Hotel. This era saw the start of mass tourism for Bali. Since ancient times, Bali had magnetized people with intellectual and spiritual inclinations, and the first prime minister of India, Jawaharlal Nehru (in office 1947–1964), described the island as "the dawn of the world." Western tourism brought international celebrities of the day, such as Noel Coward (English playwright), Charlie Chaplin (English comic actor), Barbara Hutton (a global socialite of her era from the 1930s onward), and Doris Duke (also a socialite and global heiress of the era). International celebrities helped to create an image of Bali as a modern-day Garden of Eden. By the 1970s, Australian filmmakers had started attracting multitudes of Australian visitors to Bali, specifically by producing surfing videos and building bars and nightclubs in tourist areas aimed at Australians and other international visitors.

But the lure and romance of Bali have never been without its tragedies. In 1963, Bali's only active volcano, Gunung Agung, erupted, causing at least 1,500 deaths and the evacuation of hundreds of thousands of people. Mount Agung, or the Bali Peak, rises above surrounding farmland to a height of more than 3,000 meters (9,842 feet). The volcano is known locally as "the navel of the world" and had been dormant for 120 years. Adding to the general social and political instability of the period surrounding the First World War had been a devastating earthquake in 1917, influenza that killed 22,000 people, and an atmosphere of unrest that necessitated the heightened decentralized administration of Bali. The Dutch also had altruistic reasons for empowering local negara, and they continued to support and establish the Balinese regencies toward self-rule until the start of the Second World War in 1938. These reasons included protecting Bali against harmful modernization and the threat of Islamic conversion and nationalism, which happened regardless after the close of World War II and Bali's incorporation into Indonesia. At the time, the Dutch thought that the best way to preserve and protect Balinese traditionalism was by reinvigorating the Hindu royal structures and their associated symbolism and ideologies.

When the regencies and ruling families of Bali were reinstated by the Dutch, the author of the *Babad Buleleng*, Jelantik, had his claim to the throne recognized, and he became the king of Buleleng. I Gusti Putu Jelantik (1880–1944) was a character who had been particularly skillful in ingratiating himself with the Dutch, and as the author of the infamous babad, he eventually rose to power by simultaneously building temples to prove his worth to his fellow Balinese. (Not to be confused with I Gusti Ketut Jelantik of the mid-19th century.) Unfortunately, Jelantik's rapacious desire for rulership found him alongside the colonial oppressors as a translator when they marched against other royal houses, such as Badung, Tabanan, and Klungkung, in the Dutch conquest of southern Bali. Jelantik achieved his ends, but he was not trusted by the Balinese, and his precious *Babad Buleleng* was considered a putrid work of fiction by Balinese authorities of babad.

During these campaigns, Jelantik was complicit in acquiring the holdings of the royal Balinese libraries. Along with the contents of the libraries of the royal courts of Lombok, Jelantik acquired a considerable and impressive collection of private ancient Balinese works for himself. He went on to assist the Dutch in the establishment of the manuscript library Kirtya Liefrinck-Van der Tuuk (now the Gedong Kirtya library) in Singaraja in 1928 and served as its first curator. Despite Jelantik's perceived faults, he is attributed to making a considerable effort to preserve Bali's literary heritage. The Gedong Kirtya library is on the same grounds as the Museum Buleleng and can be visited today. The library houses a collection of Dutch and Balinese works dating back to the turn of the 20th century. This *lontar* (palm leaf manuscript) library also contains *prasati* or *prasasti* (copper metal plate inscriptions) and books regarding religion, architecture, philosophy, genealogy, homeopathy, *usada* (medical scripts), and even black magic! The contents of the library are written in the old Kawi Balinese script, as well as in Dutch, German, and English. The library was established by a Dutch resident, I. J. J. Calon, a government official in Bali and Lombok during the colonial period. The library enabled extensive research on Balinese culture, customs, and language by two Dutch scholars of the same period, F. A. Liefrienk and Dr. N. van der Tuuk. Gedong Kirtya means "to endeavor to build," and this repository remains a crucial source of inspiration and information for the study of Balinese culture to this day.

The Dutch occupation of Bali occurred far later than the colonization of most of the East Indies, such as Java and the Maluku Islands, which were more sought after for commercial gain and strategic positions. Also, the Dutch hold on Bali was never as well established as those of other colonized nations. and its 20th-century domination of the island only lasted until the Japanese occupation of Bali in 1942. Batavia (Jakarta) had remained a colonial city for 320 years until 1942 when the Japanese occupied the archipelago during World War II. After the end of the war in 1945 and once Indonesia had asserted its independence, Batavia was renamed Jakarta. (In 1527, the Demak Sultanate of central Java had renamed the capital, Sunda Kelapa, to Jayakarta — "precious victory"—when it had overthrown the Majapahit Empire, from which Jakarta was eventually derived. However, the Dutch occupiers of Java had seen the capital as "Batavia.")

Imperial Japan occupied Bali during World War II with the overarching objective of forming "a Greater East Asian Co-Prosperity Sphere," aiming to liberate Eastern countries from Western domination. Future rulers of Indonesia, such as Sukarno (the first ruler of Indonesia, who also had a Balinese mother), were promoted by the Japanese, but privately, Indonesia wanted independence from both the Dutch and the Japanese. Once the Japanese troops withdrew after their surrender at the end of the war in 1945, Bali assumed independence and issued a proclamation in this regard in 1945/46. However, the Dutch were not going to give up the hard-won island so easily, and they attempted to reinstate their pre-war colonial administration, reassuming governance in the following year. The Balinese now had Japanese weapons that had been left behind by the surrendered troops in their arsenal, as well as emboldened resistance leaders, such as Colonel I Gusti Ngurah Rai. Unfortunately, Colonel Rai died as a freedom fighter in the Battle of Margarana in east Bali in 1946. The brief Balinese military resistance had been entirely obliterated by a fresh Dutch onslaught. After a short and bitter battle to assert their independence, the Balinese were once again at the mercy of foreign powers.

The Dutch denial of Balinese sovereignty resulted in tentative rule for a further four years. Bali was one of thirteen administrative districts within the newly proclaimed Dutch state of Indonesia. In the meantime, the establishment and growth of the future Republic of Indonesia (ratified on December 27th, 1949) was becoming a reality. In the immediate aftermath of World War II, an evolving Indonesia, then consisting of a number of united states, was headed by Sukarno, or Kusno Sosrodihardjo (in office 1945–1967), a Javanese politician and the first president of Indonesia, and Mohammad Hatta (in office 1945–1956), the first vice president of Indonesia. For four years, from the end of the world war to 1949, the newly formed Dutch and Indonesian contenders for the former Dutch East Indies reached a climax. Also known as the Indonesian National Revolution or the Indonesian War of Independence, this was an era of armed conflict and diplomatic struggles, as the Indonesian government fought to assert post-colonial independence. The Dutch eventually conceded in 1949 after having reached a military stalemate on the ground, specifically in Java, as well as receiving overwhelming international pressure. Bali officially became part of Indonesia in 1950, along with the other twelve island states to which the Dutch had laid claim (including the Moluccas, Java, and the Lesser Sunda Islands).

Within the same interim time period that the United States of Indonesia and the Dutch state of Indonesia were developing, the State of East Indonesia (*Negara Indonesia Timur*) was in existence. It lasted from the end of the Second World War in 1946 to the declaration of Indonesian independence, at which time it became part of Indonesia in 1950. The only president elected to the office of the State of East Indonesia was Tjokorda Gde Raka Soekawati, who was born in Ubud, Bali, in 1899 (he died in 1967). Soekawati belonged to the highest Balinese caste of Kshatriya. After a political career in Bali and Indonesia, he studied in Europe and completed his education studying agriculture in the Netherlands. Tjokorda Gde Raka Soekawati negotiated the incorporation of the State of East Indonesia into the unitary Republic of Indonesia in 1949/50. States included within the State of East Indonesia were the islands under supposed Dutch suzerainty at the time: Celebes (Sulawesi), the Moluccas, Java, Bali, and the Lesser Sundas. The Dutch approved and oversaw the regulations for the formation of the interim state, although the independent constitution of the State of East Indonesia was never implemented since it became part of the Indonesian Republic before it could be initiated. The Dutch involvement with the creation of the State of East Indonesia, which would continue to be heavily influenced by the Dutch, may have been part of a compromise by the colonialists, and Indonesians supportive of a completely independent nation criticized the formation of the state.

Bali's independence with the formation of the Republic of Indonesia was perhaps not true independence. Rajasthan (local kingdom) rule was phased out in Bali and the rest of Indonesia by the new government. The tentative Indonesian federation, consisting of a profound seventeen thousand islands, was being led by Sukarno, a revolutionary whose role had merely evolved from democracy to autocracy and finally to authoritarianism. In 1958, Bali became an official province of Indonesia, and its first governor (regional head or *kepala daerah*) was appointed, Anak Agung Bagus Suteja—the son of the last raja of Jembrana—who was in power until 1966. By 1959, Sukarno had assumed full dictatorship of the archipelago. His anti-colonial sentiments and desire to right the wrongs of Indonesia's colonial past led him increasingly toward communist sympathies. In 1963, President Sukarno resisted the concept of an Indonesian federation since it was, according to him, too suggestive of continued European rule. He was unsuccessful in this, as well as his attempt to bring the disputed territories of northern Borneo (now a part of Malaysia) into the Indonesian fold. Since the removal of Dutch colonial influence, the power of local kingdoms had been reduced, including the former Rajasthans of Bali. Being part of Indonesia did not markedly improve economic fortunes or political leverage for Bali. The Dewa Agung title lapsed with the death of the Dutch *zelfbestuurder*, Dewa Agung Oka Geg, in 1964, although members of his family have since periodically played the role of regents (*bupati*) in Klungkung.

The economic cost of Indonesia's efforts during its War of Independence resistances and subsequent failures, coupled with Sukarno's openly hostile attitude to Western powers, created hyperinflation, which lasted through most of the first half of the 1960s. The resultant social unrest and his failing health weakened President Sukarno's power base. According to Sukarno, a group of communist renegades supposedly sought out and executed eight senior generals in September of 1965 to avoid a potential military coup, although this ruse was not widely accepted. In an attempt to stabilize the government, General Suharto convinced the remaining generals to conduct a countermove, and they regained control of the military. Although Sukarno remained in power, he was rivaled by the influential and politically authoritative Suharto.

Unfortunately, the incidents of 1965 created a communist backlash in which real and suspected communists across Indonesia were hunted down and summarily killed. In this mostly unwarranted attack on real and imagined threats to the government, Bali was the scene of some of the worst atrocities. In some instances, groups of suspected communists were rounded up by mobs and clubbed to death. Half a million potential communists and ethnic Chinese lost their lives in this unnecessary cleansing, and an estimated 100,000 of these were in Bali (5 percent of Bali's population at the time). In 1966, armed soldiers removed the former Balinese governor, Anak Agung Bagus Suteja, from his house in Senayan. He was never seen again, and his political rival, under the auspices of the Indonesian National Party (PNI), claimed he had committed voluntary execution (*nyupat*) near Jakarta. Suteja had been removed from his position the previous year due to his communist sympathies and his role as the "favored son" of Sukarno. Suteja had been heavily involved in the Indonesian Revolution to expel the Dutch, and he had been imprisoned by the Dutch from 1948 to 1949 for his efforts. In 1966, in the aftermath of the communist massacres, Sukarno fled the palace and went into exile. He remained a nominal president for a further year.

Sukarno's successor, Suharto, remained in power for over three decades, and he gradually created an authoritarian kleptocracy in which he, his family, and his associates benefited the most. Suharto's military-led regime controversially enabled a sustained period of economic prosperity that lasted until the global financial crisis of 1997. Civil unrest resulting from the financial crisis, as well as general discontent due to the corrupt Indonesian leadership, led to widespread riots and violence. Ultimately, by 1999, Indonesians had ousted the incumbent Suharto and participated in their first democratic election since 1955! In 1998, the resignation of Indonesian President Suharto after thirty-two years of rulership ignited Muslim-sponsored riots by Islamists across the archipelago, including in Bali. Islamists were angered about the new government's alignment with Western powers, such as the United States, Europe, and Australia. By the time of his death, Suharto's family owned and controlled most of the prestigious resorts in Bali. The Muslim riots on Bali caused the dislocation of many Chinese and Christians whose businesses were targeted, and they subsequently had to evacuate to Lombok for safety.

Five years of tentative peace ensued for Indonesia when Suharto's daughter, President Megawati, was voted in within a provisional democracy. Although she addressed the country's legacy of corruption and its shocking human rights record, she was also governing in the aftermath of an economic crisis and general political instability. Megawati was defeated by a former military general, Susilo Bambang Yudhoyono (or SBY). SBY was Indonesia's first completely democratically elected president and served more than one term (in office 2004–2014), as his anti-corruption and moral code of honesty policies resonated with the people of Indonesia. Following SBY's term of office was the installation of the seventh and current president of Indonesia, Joko Widodo.

In 2002, two terrorist bomb attacks in the southwest tourist area of Denpasar were attributed to an Islam extremist group called Jemaah Islamiyah. The attacks were claimed to have been in retaliation for the Indonesian government's support of the United States and Australia in accordance with a transitional democratic government opening up their foreign policies. The bombs killed over two hundred people, mostly Australian tourists, and injured many more. The biggest impact of this act of terrorism was a dramatic yet expected drop in tourist numbers to Bali. Three years later, in 2005, more Islamic extremist terrorist bombings were carried out in approximately the same area, Kuta. Similar to the 2002 attacks, the perpetrators were caught and jailed or executed.

By 2010, and with the advent of the Hollywood movie *Eat Pray Love*, starring Julia Roberts (based on the book by Elizabeth Gilbert), tourism in Bali increased and began to flourish, exceeding its 2002 levels with more than two million visitors per year. Between 2010 and 2015, Bali hosted many international events, such as the 2010 International Geothermal Congress and the 2012 East Asia Summit. Bali's first elevated highway was completed during this time, as well as an upgrade to the international airport (greater Denpasar), which allowed it to manage twelve million passengers a year. The mass influx of tourists has had positive economic results and assisted with a Balinese cultural revival. However, the natural environment is said to have suffered as a result, with overdevelopment, increased environmental degradation, and pollution being common.

Unfortunately, Bali's contemporary history has been consistently punctuated by setbacks as well as successes. Mount Agung erupted again in 2017 several times, remaining active for most of the year. Residents within the danger zone were once again evacuated by the government, displacing thousands of people. Although it was mostly local families and farmers that were evacuated for several months, the eruptions negatively affected tourism for the entire year and, therefore, the entire Balinese economy. In 2018, a new governor of Bali was elected, I Wayan Koster, from Singaraja. Koster is the ninth official governor of Bali since 1950. One of the greatest negative impacts on life and socio-economic circumstances in Bali was the unforeseen COVID-19 global pandemic. An estimated 5,000 people have lost their lives due to the disease so far, and the Balinese government closed all international travel. For a small developing island state that draws 80 percent of its economy from tourism and related sectors, the pandemic had a devastating effect on the island both economically and socially.

Chapter 9 – Existing Heritage

In 1901, the Dutch introduced the Ethical Policy, which sought to expand educational opportunities for indigenous peoples in the East Indies. They were eager to prove that their influence in the archipelago could not be equated with the extractive scramble of other European powers. Also, shortly after the 1906–1908 campaigns against the Balinese, the Dutch portrayal by the Western press was becoming increasingly negative, and they sought to correct these perceptions. Amongst other things, the Ethical Policy resulted in the establishment of universities in Jakarta during the first half of the 20th century, which still exist today, albeit under new names. The Ethical Policy claimed to be repaying a "debt of honor" for the wealth that they had drawn from the East Indies over the centuries. They sought to bring "peace, order, and modernity" to the indigenous peoples of the East Indies and to free them from the "tyrannous" rule of the monarchies. Along with the Ethical Policy, the Dutch began promoting tourism in about 1914 in an effort to display Bali as a "living museum" of preserved culture. These efforts by the Dutch were known as the "Balinization" of Bali.

True urban nodes (small cities) did not develop until the mid-19th century on Bali, with the influence of the Dutch, and the Balinese never experienced the mass urbanization that was common to people of medieval Europe. Overall, Balinese life is communal and centers largely on religion. Its modern-day religions include Balinese Hinduism, Buddhism, Malay ancestor cult, and animistic and magical beliefs and practices. The Balinese people also firmly believe in reincarnation. Muslims and Christians, as well as Chinese, also live in Bali, mostly in the west and north of the island. Known as "the Island of the Gods" or "Island of a Thousand Puras (Temples)," Bali is home to an abundance of places of worship. There are in excess of twenty thousand Balinese Hindu temples on the island, each dedicated to a particular aspect of life or Balinese spiritual geography. Balinese Hinduism developed from Shaivite Hinduism as well as Buddhism, which were brought to Bali throughout the island's history. Since Hindu practices are more focused on a spiritual way of life than a specific dogma, a unique type of Hinduism arose and flourished in Bali, outlasting the 16th-century Islamic conversion that was typical of the rest of Indonesia.

This Balinese Hinduism adopted the cultural style of the Balinese, who are enthusiastic about mixing ancient religious philosophies and ideas, as well as myths and legends, with modern-day festivities, arts, and traditions. Not long after Indonesia's independence in 1949, the Balinese needed to fight for the recognition of their unique island religion, and finally, in 1959, Balinese Hinduism was established as one of Indonesia's official faiths. Balinese Hinduism is a unique combination of Mahayana Buddhism and Shaivite Hinduism. The adherents of the religion only believe in one god—*Sang Hyang Widhi*, *Acintya*, or *Sang Hyang Tunggal*—although the followers still worship various forms of this god and continue with animistic rituals in daily life. Balinese Hinduism can also be referred to as Shiva-Buddhism, Hindu-Dharma, Tirtha religions, or the Holy Water Religion. The most important aspect of Balinese Hinduism is that its adherents find the spiritual meaning of their lives and the attainment of perfection through *moksha* (becoming one with the universe). The religion is not based on a prescribed doctrine but is more of a personal experience that draws from the ancient spiritual traditions and scriptures of Nusantara.

Although the Hindu caste system is observed in Bali, it is less socially entrenched than in places such as mainland India. The main reason for equality in Bali is that most of the population belongs to the lowest (Sudra / Shudra) caste. However, noble classes do exist in the form of priests (Brahman), the military and royal classes (Kshatriya), and merchants (Vaishya). Intermarriages across castes are not readily accepted (known as the practice of endogamy). The modern-day Balinese language is distinct from that of east Java, from which most of the Balinese culture developed, but upper-class Balinese contains many Javanese as well as Sanskrit words.

Balinese villages all contain temples, as well as assembly halls, which are usually located on a square that hosts markets and festivals. Families live in compounds surrounded by natural walls. Each village has its own orchestral club, and pantomimes (stage plays) and traditional dancing are a significant part of Balinese life. These plays serve as important sources of passing on indigenous knowledge through stories or preserving magico-religious beliefs. The Wayang puppet theater is thought to have lasted until modern times because the puppeteers have acted as teachers of history and have also played a crucial role in communicating key political and cultural ideas. Wayang is an intrinsic part of the indigenous culture of Bali, in addition to being an art form and a method of entertainment. The show is often accompanied by a local choir or orchestra. Wayang has grown over the centuries to include all Balinese art forms (visual and performance) and continues to evolve. It remains an important medium for information-sharing, teaching, preaching, philosophizing, and entertainment.

Balinese temples, aside from their religious, cultural, and community value, are timeless pieces that represent the lost empires of Bali. Dating from the early Indianized kingdoms through the Majapahit era and into the 20th century, the temples and shrines (and sometimes homes) of Bali provide a constant reminder of the island's exotic, spiritual past. Many of the temples exist in layers, as each new generation and culture added their additions and influences to these revered structures. Unfortunately, numerous palaces, such as the Klungkung Palace, were destroyed by the Dutch colonizers in the 1800s and 1900s, and these have been replaced since then, albeit in the traditional Balinese style. An example of ancient architecture on Bali are the towering paduraksa (or kori) gateways to temples—a multilayered roofed structure adorning the entrance archway, very typical of temples on Java and Bali.

The Balinese are extremely fond of music, poetry, dancing, and festivals. A Balinese orchestra (*gamelan, gamelang,* or *gamelin*) is the traditional music ensemble of Java, Bali, and the Sundas and an integral part of local Balinese culture. The gamelan usually consists of a multitude of percussion instruments (specifically metallophones, metal drums, and gongs, amongst others), two-string violins, and bamboo flutes. The gamelan can be accompanied by male and female vocalists as well. The Balinese people are supremely talented in arts and crafts and regularly indulge in betting games such as cockfighting. Bali's widespread artistic temperament is evident in their painting, sculpture, metalworking (gold, silver, and bronze smithing), spinning and weaving, musical instruments, and wood and bone carving. Even funerals are associated with beauty and festivities in Bali, and processions of flower-covered mourners accompany the dead, who lay in animal-shaped wooden coffins, to the cremation grounds. Bali painting and sculpture have been heavily influenced by the Hindu religion, as their purpose was mostly to inspire ethical values relating to the laws of adat (traditional law). In early Balinese painting, colorful two-dimensional drawings were done on cloth or bark paper. These paintings were of a distinctly religious inclination and were produced anonymously for temples and royal palaces. By the 20th century, the influx of visitors and Western artists allowed for more paintings that represented Balinese life rather than religious concepts, and they had a more commercial value as objects of art for tourists.

The foundation of Balinese performing arts is folk dancing and gamelan music, which are taught to young children by villagers. These highly stylized performances tell stories of ancient legends and are used to represent each individual's right of passage or other celebrations for the Balinese. The dance culture is a natural expression of Balinese religious beliefs brought to life through exaggerated, angular movements coordinated with intense eye, hand, and arm placements. Most of the dances involve the tyrannical character of the witch (demon queen), Rangda, who personifies the dark forces of the Balinese mythological kingdom. The Barong (Chinese-orientated lion beast) is also a common feature of a dance performance and represents the force for good. The constant contest between Rangda and the Barong represents the continual fight between good and evil for the Balinese. The dancers (usually girls) are dressed in colorful brocades of indigenous dress with tall, stylized gold-colored headpieces with heavy makeup and bold ornaments. Some Balinese dance is not religiously orientated and serves simply for celebrations and entertainment. The Balinese dances can also include a trance-like state by the dancers when benevolent spirits are believed to inhabit their bodies.

The Balinese living tradition of folk dance, showing girls in the Pendet *(greeting) dance.*

The Balinese artistic temperament was significantly influenced by the late 15th-century influx of Hindu intellectuals, literati, artists, and spiritualists after the collapse of the Majapahit Empire. This original series of influxes may have been the root cause for the Balinese ability to merge fact with fiction, history with literature, religion with folklore, and modern political maneuvering with ancestral power. For instance, the babad (Balinese chronicles) are considered more than legendary historical records. These textual heirlooms, or *pusaka*, embody monarchical and supernatural authority. The babad link ancestors from the past with the life and times of the present and ambitions for the future. Since nothing in Bali seems to be outside of the power of Saraswati, the Hindu goddess of arts and literature, the babad are part of the religious and artistic culture of the Balinese as well and are often interned, along with other items of court regalia, in shrines and temples. One feature of Balinese entertainment and culture is the recital of babad and their exemplification in performing arts, such as the Wayang puppet theater.

Bali has unfortunately inherited a legacy of earthquakes and volcanic eruptions, with the latest seismic events occurring in 2018. The most detrimental effect of these natural disasters is the disruptive influence they have on everyday life, causing some of the population to be relocated. Tourism continues to draw millions of visitors each year to Bali, and they are intent upon enjoying the beaches and ocean, the nightlife, and the Balinese culture. The Balinese have developed their indigenous performing arts as well as crafts and handiwork to keep abreast of the demand by foreigners for their unique civilization. Klungkung, in the southeast and including Bali's three smaller satellite islands, is well-known for wood carving and its gold and silver industries, which are largely supplied by mines from Sumatra and Java. The ability to work with precious metals was brought by Majapahit smiths from Java and possibly from the Chinese Dong Son people during the Bronze Age. Today, most of Bali's silversmithing is centered around the village of Celuk, where metalworking skills stretch back for many generations. *Songket* (traditional Indonesian) textiles and pottery can be found in modern-day Gelgel. Exquisite baskets echoing the Austronesian craftsmanship are manufactured in the Bali Aga village of Tenganan. Gianyar's lively market, as well as the tourist destinations of Kuta, Sanur, and Nusa Dua (beachside locales in the south), draw many foreign visitors. Ubud, farther north in the foothills of Bali, is a center for international artists and includes the Agung Rai Museum of Art.

Although Indonesia does not recognize the Balinese royal kingdoms or their unofficial powers, some of these lineages exist in pockets across Bali and are adhered to within the communities, mostly through adherence to the caste class hierarchy. The ancestors of Balinese royal houses know who they are and from whom they are descended, and they sometimes enjoy special privileges, such as palatial homes. Bali's demographics are constituted of a mix of cultures originating from population influxes from different lands over millennia. Modern-day Bali consists of almost 90 percent ethnic Balinese, and the remaining groups—often distinguished by country of origin or religion—largely live separately from the traditional Balinese. As an example, the Aga Balinese, who originally crossed over from Java in the 8ᵗʰ century, now live in secluded isolation in the mountainous regions of Bali. The distinct tribes that developed as part of the Bali Aga are separated into a number of villages around the foot of Gunung Agung and have developed their own dialects of Balinese. The Bali Aga resist all forms of outside influence, and they prefer to maintain their removed societies according to *awig-awig* (customary rules). The Bali Agas' strict marital codes prevent marriage outside the community unless the person leaves the community and also prohibits divorce and polygamy. This isolation and the Agas' strict perpetuation of ancient customs have created communities preserved in time, which allow a glimpse into the past of what original Austronesian communities may have been like. From ancient cotton-dyeing techniques to uniquely Aga architecture, the Bali Aga continue to stand proudly and determinedly separate from the Balinese of the lowlands, who now freely mix with foreign tourists, although two Bali Aga villages now allow tourists to visit. Aga tourism is centered around artistry, festivities, and unique products, such as traditional geringsing fabric. The Bali Aga still celebrate the arrival of their ancestors of old in traditional Balinese fashion with music, dance, and artistry.

About a quarter of Bali's farmland is irrigated, and this is used mainly for rice. Other crops include coffee, yams, oil palms, cassava, corn, coconuts, and other fruits. Farmers raise cattle as well as smaller livestock. Surprisingly, fishing remains a minor occupation for the local communities. Unusually, the Balinese agricultural system is linked to their penchant for spiritual rituals and folk art. Bali's flourishing rice cultivation system and rich, fertile soils have ensured the population's supply of food for millennia and also provided excess for trade. This abundance of a staple food source has allowed the Balinese the time and energy to participate in and develop their numerous art forms and spiritual pursuits. In a world of rapidly changing ideals, the Balinese still employ the process of communal decision-making or *musyawarah*. The rice paddies are a communal affair (*gotong-royong*), which include in-built irrigation systems that channel water collected by the forests of higher altitudes. The terraced paddies are connected via a system of canals, weirs, and tunnels, and the workforce to maintain the paddies is drawn from local communities, who use hand tools to cultivate and harvest the rice.

Balinese rice terraces at Jatiluwih, one of the five rice terraces of the subak irrigation system and a UNESCO World Heritage Site.

Alfred Russel Wallace, a British explorer, had this to say about Bali when landing at Singaraja in 1860 after departing from Singapore:

> I was both astonished and delighted; for as my visit to Java was some years later, I had never beheld so beautiful and well-cultivated a district out of Europe. A slightly undulating plain extends from the seacoast about ten or twelve miles inland, where it is bounded by a fine range of wooded and cultivated hills. Houses and villages, marked out by dense clumps of coconut palms, tamarind and other fruit trees, are dotted about in every direction; while between them extend luxurious rice-grounds, watered by an elaborate system of irrigation that would be the pride of the best cultivated parts of Europe.

It seems that Bali's landscape has not changed significantly since Wallace's time. Strangely, the Balinese have never been keen seafarers or coastal navigators. The unusually treacherous approach to Bali via sea contributed to the island's ability to "turn its back on the world" as the mountainous north created a natural land barrier to passing maritime traders, not to mention its ports have always been small and few. Instead, Balinese attention is turned inward to their island home, and Balinese spirituality and cosmology are inseparably bound up with their beautiful land. The unique Balinese Hinduism is a combination of Hinduism, Buddhism, and Tantra (the esoteric aspects of both religions), as well as local indigenous beliefs and ancestor cult worship, nature worship, and animism. The three realms of the Balinese belief system might explain why they have never been avid seafarers. Higher powers are believed to occupy the higher realm of the mountains and skies (the *hyang* spirits), humans live in the interim world, and dark forces are ever-present below the depths of the sea. The sometimes frenetic worship and attendance at multiple temples reflect their beliefs that their island is constituted of gods, demons, and people and that it is their responsibility to manage these complex arrangements of entities.

The Balinese concept of Tri Hita Karana is one that brings together the realms of spirit, humanity, and nature in the pursuit of well-being and prosperity. Tri Hita Karana is similar to the Western idea of "sustainable development" and also includes unique alignments of entrances and structures (similar to the Eastern concept of feng shui) in all Balinese buildings, specifically the temples. But these spiritual ideologies are not confined to only buildings, and the complexities of Balinese Hinduism are included in each and every aspect of their lives, from the building of temples and homes to clothing, eating, dancing, and all forms of expression in an attempt to create a balance of life forces (*rwa bhineda*) on the island and amongst its people. There is no dedicated holy day in the weekly lives of the Balinese because every day is sacred and filled with numerous offerings to the gods, ceremonies, processions, and the burning of fragrant incenses. The local offerings, or *kriya bebali*, which are not only transient offerings and handmade objects but also permanent stone works and sculptures for the temples and shrines, are an expression of the Balinese collective life. Rituals and the social environment of Bali are inseparable, and the Balinese constantly put their aesthetic and communal efforts toward achieving balance.

The Balinese use art and beautifully created objects as a common visual language, and their talents have tied in well to the tourist industry through which the Balinese can sell their works and handicrafts. Art is such an important part of Balinese life that they don't define arts and crafts as separate acts because they are a part of their daily routine. The closest concept to sacred visual arts is *kriya bebali*, or "craft offerings." *Kriya* is crucial to the identity and culture of Bali (and Indonesia as a whole). Daily artistic creations and spiritual offerings are done regularly and do not necessarily last long. Natively, these offerings are called *kriya becik*, which translates as "complete, beautiful, and sacred." Village women carry piles of fruit on their heads to be blessed at the temple each day, palm leaves are woven into *lamak* (long hangings for rituals at shrines), and funeral towers for parades are all dispensable and can be burned or eaten soon afterward. Balinese arts, crafts, and sculptures are considered a method of honoring god or the gods on a daily basis. For the Balinese, beauty and the divine are a single concept that is the core of life and not separate abstract concepts that are apportioned certain hours in the week. In fact, the Hindu-based Balinese calendar is an expression of ten simultaneous cycles so that each day of the 210-day year can be defined by ten different names. Although the Balinese also use a solar/lunar calendar similar to the Western Gregorian calendar, it is not designed to numericize or stipulate a specific point in time as Westerners do. Both the Hindu (Pawukon) and the lunar (saka) Balinese calendars emphasize a more fluid sense of time, understood by the Balinese as the "motionless present."

The most unusual facet of Balinese religious worship, which is no different from their sense of "being" or "living," is that it has survived unchanged throughout the duration of Bali's history. Bali's parent country, Indonesia, is currently the world's largest Muslim majority country, but they still retain the symbol of their Hindu/Buddhist origins through the eagle-like Garuda bird as their national identity. Within three hundred years of the Dutch arrival in Nusantara (the early 1600s), Islam had become the method by which indigenous populations resisted colonialism. Islam continued to strengthen within Indonesia into the 20th century, and the Malay Archipelago's Islamic state exchanges with other Muslim countries grew stronger into the modern era. Bali's resistance to Islam and its perpetuation of the unique Balinese Hinduism has made the island vulnerable to Islamic terrorist attacks. The more Bali attracts foreign visitors from "the Western world," the more Islamic extremists estimate that Bali is aligning with foreign, non-Islamist societies. Terrorism remains an ongoing threat to the island, but Bali continues unchanged in culture and religion as it has done for at least the last millennium. The island has submitted to the waves of change that have inevitably engulfed this small, remote state within an immense archipelago. The constant influx of foreign powers or curious visitors still leaves Balinese resolute that they and the paradise they call home are unique and should remain so.

Conclusion

Bali is the most intriguing of the Indonesian archipelagic jewels of maritime Southeast Asia. It is a small, unique island, but it is big enough to draw the attention of migrants, invaders, and colonizers over thousands of years. Throughout Bali's history, the island has enjoyed an intriguing position within the Malay Archipelago trade routes. As Bali is closely neighboring Java and near to the Spice Islands, it has been submitted time and again to foreign rule as its people were forced to subjugate themselves to powers greater than themselves. Described as a nation of "aesthetes," the peaceful, spiritual, and culturally colorful societies that constitute Bali could not compete with the ambitions and interests of subcontinental India, Java, and Europe. In Bali's early history, the people took little action in repelling external forces and the endless waves of cultural and economic changes that engulfed their paradise. The Balinese adapted, integrated new cultures, and waited for each new independence that inevitably followed foreign rule.

During Bali's more modern history of the colonial period, the tragedy of the island's vulnerability caught up with it. Having been protected for hundreds of years from out-and-out exploitation, plunder, and colonization, it finally fell to the Dutch at the turn of the 20th century. Bali's lack of spices and other commodities for trade had kept the island safe from archipelagic interlopers that had harvested and plundered the East Indies for centuries. But the Dutch, who controlled so much of Indonesia and Java, would not rest until they completed their colonial arsenal of archipelagic control. The indigenous kingdoms of Bali, which traced their heritage back to the mesmerizing Majapahit Empire, were irrevocably dismantled. In a quick succession of uncontrollable circumstances, Dutch domination gave way to Japanese occupation during the Second World War, followed by Indonesia's overall claim of the former Dutch East Indies. Bali was swallowed up as a province of a far greater archipelagic republic, which remains its current status.

The island of Bali never entirely submitted to foreign powers, but it has also never been completely independent for any significant period of time. It has most often existed as a vassal state of a greater nation and dutifully incorporated different cultures, religions, and socio-political systems into its multifarious existence. In its current status as a province of the Republic of Indonesia, Bali is the only Hindu majority state of the Muslim-dominated island chain. Soon after its provincial independence, Bali had to fight for recognition of the unique Balinese Hinduism for which it is known—an eclectic blend of Buddhism, Hinduism, and other indigenous belief systems. The Balinese royal houses are still not recognized by its parent Indonesia in any official capacity, and the island's present echoes its past struggle for sovereignty or at least an individualized state identity.

Well-known historians herald Bali as an example of the extinguished Indo-Javanese societies of old. Bali is a living monument that celebrates the golden age of Hindu-Buddhist maritime empires that ruled the seas of Southeast Asia in pursuit of spices, exotic goods, and, most importantly, the sharing of philosophies and spiritual ideologies. Exemplifying a magnificent blend of ethnicities, cultures, and creeds, Bali continues as a timeless example of a magical and heroic past that evolved into the sublime, heterogenous tourist hotspot of today, one that is visited and loved by people from around the world for its singularity and faithful adherence to the past.

Here's another book by Captivating History that you might like

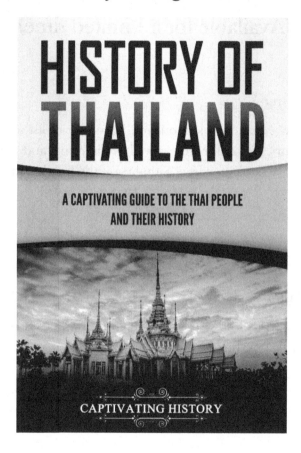

Free Bonus from Captivating History
(Available for a Limited time)

Hi History Lovers!

Now you have a chance to join our exclusive history list so you can get your first history ebook for free as well as discounts and a potential to get more history books for free! Simply visit the link below to join.

Captivatinghistory.com/ebook

Also, make sure to follow us on Facebook, Twitter and Youtube by searching for Captivating History.

References

Bali.com: *Bali's History: The History of Island of the Gods,* https://bali.com/bali-travel-guide/culture-religion-traditions/balinese-history/, accessed February, March 2021,

Hinduism in Bali, https://bali.com/bali-travel-guide/culture-religion-traditions/balinese-hinduism-religion/, accessed February, March 2021.

Baliaround.com: *Barong Landung: Balinese Legend,* https://www.baliaround.com/barong-landung/, accessed February, March 2021.

Bellwood, Peter, et al., editors. *Austronesian Prehistory in Southeast Asia: Homeland, Expansion and Transformation.* The Austronesians: Historical and Comparative Perspectives, ANU Press, 2006, pp. 103–118, accessed via *JSTOR,* www.jstor.org/stable/j.ctt2jbjx1.8, February, March 2021.

Britannica: *Austronesian Languages,* https://www.britannica.com/topic/Austronesian-languages, accessed February, March 2021,

Bali, https://www.britannica.com/place/Bali-island-and-province-Indonesia, accessed February, March 2021,

Dong Son Culture, https://www.britannica.com/topic/Dong-Son-culture, accessed February, March 2021,

East Indies, https://www.britannica.com/place/East-Indies, accessed February, March 2021,:*Indonesia*, https://www.britannica.com/place/Indonesia, accessed February, March 2021.

DiscoverBaliIndonesia.com: *Balinese Arts and Crafts*, http://www.discover-bali-indonesia.com/encyclopedia-balinese-art-craft.html, accessed February, March 2021,

Balinese Calendar, http://www.discover-bali-indonesia.com/encyclopedia-balinese-calendar.html, accessed February, March 2021,

Balinese Cosmology, http://www.discover-bali-indonesia.com/encyclopedia-balinese-cosmology.html, accessed February, March 2021.

Farram, Steve, 1998. *The Dutch Conquest of Bali: The Conspiracy Theory Revisited, Indonesia and the Malay World*, 26:76, 207-223, DOI:10.1080/13639819908729924 accessed via www.tandfonline.com, February, March 2021.

Frommer's.com. *History in Bali*, https://www.frommers.com/destinations/bali/in-depth/history, accessed February, March 2021.

Guampedia.com, 2019. *Canoe Building*, https://www.guampedia.com/canoe-building-2/, accessed February, March 2021.

Gunadi, Ari. *Besakih Temple in Bali*, accessed via Hotels.com, https://au.hotels.com/go/indonesia/besakih-temple, February, March 2021.

Gunther, Michael D., http://www.art-and-archaeology.com/indonesia/indonesia.html, accessed February, March 2021.

Hagerdal, Hans, 1995. *Bali in the Sixteenth and Seventeenth Centuries: Suggestions for a Chronology of the Gelgel Period.* Bijdragen Tot De Taal-, Land- En Volkenkunde, vol. 151, no. 1, 1995, pp. 101–124, accessed via *JSTOR,* www.jstor.org/stable/27864631, February, March 2021.

Kalpavriksha, 2019. *Dang Hyang Nirartha, Reformer of the Indonesian Dharma,* accessed via https://medium.com/@Kalpavriksha/dang-hyang-nirartha-reformer-of-the-indonesian-dharma-26ac19dbea8c, February, March 2021.

Kapil, Iris. Iris Sans Frontieres Blog:

Rice and Slavery in Colonial America, 2018, https://irissansfrontieres.wordpress.com/category/bali/, accessed February, March 2021,

The Artful Crafts of Bali, Part 1, 2016, https://irissansfrontieres.wordpress.com/2016/12/03/the-artful-crafts-of-bali-part-i/, accessed February, March 2021,

The Artful Crafts of Bali, Part 2, 2017, https://irissansfrontieres.wordpress.com/2017/01/01/the-artful-crafts-of-bali-part-ii/, accessed February, March 2021,

The Artful Crafts of Bali, Part 3, 2017, https://irissansfrontieres.wordpress.com/2017/01/31/the-artful-crafts-of-bali-part-iii/, accessed February, March 2021.

Lalor, Ailish, 2020. *What was the VOC? The Dutch East India Company Explained,* accessed via DutchReview.com, https://dutchreview.com/culture/history/voc-dutch-east-india-company-explained/, February, March 2021.

Lansing, J. Stephen et. al., 2001. *Volcanic fertilization of Balinese rice paddies,* accessed via Elsevier, Ecological Economics 38 (2001) 383 – 390.

Lonelyplanet.com: :*Gelgel,* https://www.lonelyplanet.com/indonesia/klungkung-

semarapura/attractions/gelgel/a/poi-sig/1554081/1002205, accessed
February, March 2021.

Mahavidya, *The Sanjaya Dynasty*,
http://www.mahavidya.ca/2012/06/18/the-sanjaya-dynasty/, accessed
February, March 2021.

National Geographic:

Rutledge et. al., 2011. *Monsoon*,
https://www.nationalgeographic.org/encyclopedia/monsoon/, accessed
February, March

2021.

Newworldencyclopedia.org: :*Majapahit*,
https://www.newworldencyclopedia.org/entry/Majapahit, accessed
February, March 2021.

NowBali.co.id: :*Mads Lange: Why a Danish Man has a Kuta street
named after him*,

https://nowbali.co.id/mads-lange-bali-history/, accessed February,
March 2021.

NusaStudio, *Balinese Silver-making*, https://www.nusa.studio/balinese-
silver/, accessed February, March 2021.

Rivers, P.J., 2004. *Monsoon Rhythms and Trade Patterns: Ancient
Times East of Suez.* Journal of the Malaysian Branch of the Royal
Asiatic Society Vol.77, No.2 (287) (2004), pp.59-93, *JSTOR*,
https://www.jstor.org/stable/41493525?read-
now=1&seq=1#page_scan_tab_contents, accessed February, March
2021.

Speake, Jennifer, 2003. *Literature of Travel and Exploration: G to P*,
accessed via Google Books, February, March 2021.

Sunarya, I Ketut, 2021. *Kriya Bebali in Bali: its essence, symbolic,
aesthetic*, accessed via tandfonline.com,
https://doi.org/10.1080/23311886.2021.1882740, February, March
2021.

Thomas, Prof. David R., 2011, *Origins of the Austronesian Peoples*, University of Auckland, New Zealand, accessed via ResearchGate, https://www.researchgate.net/publication/236169876_Origins_of_the_ Austronesian_Peoples, February, March 2021.

Tatu, Robin, 1999. *I Gusti Putu Jelantik's Babad Buleleng Placed within Historical Context*, Explorations in Southeast Asian Studies, A Journal of the Southeast Asian Studies Student Association, Vol 3, accessed via the University of Hawaii, https://scholarspace.manoa.hawaii.edu/bitstream/10125/2540/1/I%20 Gusti%20Putu%20Jelantik%27s%20Babad%20Buleleng%20Placed%2 0within%20Histori.pdf, February, March 2021.

Tripati, S., 2017. *HISTORICAL NOTES, Early users of monsoon winds for navigation,* accessed via ResearchGate, https://www.researchgate.net/publication/321418755_HISTORICAL _NOTES_Early_users_of_monsoon_winds_for_navigation, February, March 2021.

Villa-Bali.com: *What's Behind the Name Bali,* https://www.villa-bali.com/guide/whats-bali/, accessed February, March 2021.

VisitBali.id. *Bali Aga Tribe: Indigenous People of Bali,* https://visitbali.id/property/the-bali-aga-of-trunyan-traditional-village, accessed February, March 2021.

Wikipedia: *Airlangga,* https://en.wikipedia.org/wiki/Airlangga, accessed February, March 2021,

Anak Agung Bagus Suteja, https://en.wikipedia.org/wiki/Anak_Agung_Bagus_Suteja, accessed February, March 2021,

Anglurah Agung, https://en.wikipedia.org/wiki/Anglurah_Agung, accessed February, March 2021,

Austronesian Peoples, https://en.wikipedia.org/wiki/Austronesian_peoples, accessed February, March 2021,

Bali, https://en.wikipedia.org/wiki/Bali, accessed February, March 2021,

Bali Kingdom, https://en.wikipedia.org/wiki/Bali_Kingdom, accessed February, March 2021, :*Bali Temple*, https://en.wikipedia.org/wiki/Balinese_temple, accessed February, March 2021,

Balinese Dance, https://en.wikipedia.org/wiki/Balinese_dance, accessed February, March 2021,

Batavia, Dutch East Indies, https://en.wikipedia.org/wiki/Batavia,_Dutch_East_Indies, accessed February, March 2021,

Colin McPhee, https://en.wikipedia.org/wiki/Colin_McPhee, accessed February, March 2021,

Coral Triangle, https://en.wikipedia.org/wiki/Coral_Triangle, accessed February, March 2021, *Dang Hyang Nirartha*, https://en.wikipedia.org/wiki/Dang_Hyang_Nirartha, accessed February, March 2021,

Dewa Agung, https://en.wikipedia.org/wiki/Dewa_Agung, accessed February, March 2021, *Dutch East India Company*, https://en.wikipedia.org/wiki/Dutch_East_India_Company, accessed February, March 2021,

Dutch Intervention in Bali (1906), https://en.wikipedia.org/wiki/Dutch_intervention_in_Bali_(1906), accessed February, March 2021,

Dutch Intervention in Bali (1849), https://en.wikipedia.org/wiki/Dutch_intervention_in_Bali_(1849), accessed February, March 2021,

Dutch Intervention in Lombok, https://en.wikipedia.org/wiki/Dutch_intervention_in_Lombok_and_K arangasem, accessed February, March 2021,

East India Company,
https://en.wikipedia.org/wiki/East_India_Company, accessed
February, March 2021,

Geringsing, https://en.wikipedia.org/wiki/Geringsing, accessed
February, March 2021,

History of Bali, https://en.wikipedia.org/wiki/History_of_Bali,
accessed February, March 2021,

Flora of Indonesia,
https://en.wikipedia.org/wiki/Flora_of_Indonesia#Sundaland,
accessed February, March 2021,

French and British interregnum in the Dutch East Indies,
https://en.wikipedia.org/wiki/French_and_British_interregnum_in_the
_Dutch_East_Indies, accessed February, March 2021,

Gelgel, Indonesia, https://en.wikipedia.org/wiki/Gelgel,_Indonesia,
accessed February, March 2021,

Gregory Bateseon, https://en.wikipedia.org/wiki/Gregory_Bateson,
accessed February, March 2021,

Indonesian National Revolution,
https://en.wikipedia.org/wiki/Indonesian_National_Revolution,
accessed February, March 2021,

Islam in Indonesia,
https://en.wikipedia.org/wiki/Islam_in_Indonesia#History, accessed
February, March 2021,

Jakarta, https://en.wikipedia.org/wiki/Jakarta, accessed February,
March 2021,

Kakawin, https://en.wikipedia.org/wiki/Kakawin, February, March
2021,

Kakawin Sutasoma, https://en.wikipedia.org/wiki/Kakawin_Sutasoma,
accessed February, March 2021,

Lesser Sunda Islands,
https://en.wikipedia.org/wiki/Lesser_Sunda_Islands, accessed
February, March 2021,

Lombok, https://en.wikipedia.org/wiki/Lombok#History, accessed
February, March 2021,

Mads Johansen Lange,
https://en.wikipedia.org/wiki/Mads_Johansen_Lange, accessed
February, march 2021,

Maluku Islands, https://en.wikipedia.org/wiki/Maluku_Islands,
accessed February, March 2021,

Margaret Mead, https://en.wikipedia.org/wiki/Margaret_Mead,
accessed February, March 2021,

Mataram Sultanate, https://en.wikipedia.org/wiki/Mataram_Sultanate,
accessed February, March 2021,

Medang Kingdom, https://en.wikipedia.org/wiki/Medang_Kingdom,
accessed February, March 2021,

Miguel Covarrubias,
https://en.wikipedia.org/wiki/Miguel_Covarrubias, accessed February,
March 2021,

Moon of Pejeng, https://en.wikipedia.org/wiki/Moon_of_Pejeng,
accessed February, March 2021,

Nagarakretagama, https://en.wikipedia.org/wiki/Nagarakretagama,
accessed February, march 2021,

Nusantara, https://en.wikipedia.org/wiki/Nusantara, accessed
February, March 2021,

Pejeng Drum, https://en.wikipedia.org/wiki/Pejeng_drum, accessed
February, March 2021, *Portuguese Malacca,*
https://en.wikipedia.org/wiki/Portuguese_Malacca, accessed February,
March 2021,

Provinces of Indonesia,
https://en.wikipedia.org/wiki/Provinces_of_Indonesia, accessed
February, March 2021,

Ring of Fire, https://en.wikipedia.org/wiki/Ring_of_Fire, accessed
February, March 2021,:*Shailendra Dynasty,*
https://en.wikipedia.org/wiki/Shailendra_dynasty, accessed February,
March 2021,

Singaraja, https://en.wikipedia.org/wiki/Singaraja, accessed February,
March 2021,

Singhasari, https://en.wikipedia.org/wiki/Singhasari, accessed
February, March 2021,

Sir Stamford Raffles, https://en.wikipedia.org/wiki/Stamford_Raffles,
accessed February, March 2021,

Spanish East Indies,
https://en.wikipedia.org/wiki/Spanish_East_Indies, accessed February,
March 2021,

Spice Trade, https://en.wikipedia.org/wiki/Spice_trade, accessed
February, March 2021,

Sunda Shelf, https://en.wikipedia.org/wiki/Sunda_Shelf, accessed
February, March 2021,

Tjokorda Gde Raka Soekawati,
https://en.wikipedia.org/wiki/Tjokorda_Gde_Raka_Soekawati,
accessed February, March 2021, *Trade Route,*
https://en.wikipedia.org/wiki/Trade_route, accessed February, March
2021, *Wayang,* https://en.wikipedia.org/wiki/Wayang, accessed
February, March 2021, *Wallace Line,*
https://en.wikipedia.org/wiki/Wallace_Line, accessed February,
March 2021, *Walter Spies,*
https://en.wikipedia.org/wiki/Walter_Spies, accessed February, March
2021.

WonderfulBali.com: :*Lontar Library Gedong Kirtya Singaraja,*
https://www.wonderfulbali.com/lontar-library-gedong-kirtya-singaraja/,
accessed February, March 2021.

Image References

[1] Physical Map of Indonesia. *Source:* Worldometers, *https://www.worldometers.info/img/maps/indonesia_physical_map.gif,* accessed February, March 2021.

[2] Map of Lesser Sunda Islands. *Source:* Lencer, 2017. Accessed via Wikimedia Commons, *https://commons.wikimedia.org/wiki/File:Lesser_Sunda_Islands_en.png,* accessed February, March 2021.

[3] Bali Topography Map. *Source:* Bali Tourism Board, *https://www.balitourismboard.org/bali_topolgraphy.html,* accessed February, March 2021.

[4] The Ubud Monkey Sanctuary. *Source:* Deepti Gupta, Travel Triangle, https://traveltriangle.com/blog/ubud-monkey-forest/, accessed February, March 2021.

[5] Austronesian Prau. *Source:* Guampedia, 2019, *Canoe Building,* https://www.guampedia.com/canoe-building-2/, accessed February, March 2021.

[6] Neolithic Stone Sarcophagus. *Source:* World Imaging, 2009, accessed via Wikimedia Commons, https://commons.wikimedia.org/wiki/File:Neolithic_stone_sarcophagus_Bali.jpg, February, March 2021.

[7] Pejeng Drum. *Source*: Wikiwand, Pejeng Drum, https://www.wikiwand.com/en/Pejeng_drum, accessed February, March 2021.

[8] Women in Geringsing clothe. *Source*: Bewishbaliblog, 'Bali Culture Advisor', 2016, https://balicultureadvisor.wordpress.com/2016/04/21/gringsing-cloth/, accessed February, March 2021.

[9] Jagatnatha Temple, Jembrana. *Source:* Sunarya, 2011, pg. 235, accessed via Taylor & Francis Online. Sunarya, I Ketut, 2021, *Kriya Bebali in Bali: Its essence, symbolic, and aesthetic,* https://www.tandfonline.com/doi/full/10.1080/23311886.2021.1882740, accessed February, March 2021.

[10] Besakih Temple Bali. *Source:* CEphoto, Uwe Aranas, 2015 accessed via Wikimedia Commons, https://commons.wikimedia.org/wiki/File:Besakih_Bali_Indonesia_Pura-Besakih-02.jpg, and https://commons.wikimedia.org/wiki/File:Besakih_Bali_Indonesia_Pura-Besakih-01.jpg, February, March 2021.

[11] Rambut Siwi Temple. *Source*: BaliFantastic.com, https://www.balifantastic.com/tourism-objects/rambut-siwi-temple/, February, March 2021.

[12] Balinese Pendet Dance. *Source*: Michel, Christopher, 2009, accessed via Wikimedia Commons, https://commons.wikimedia.org/wiki/File:Tari_Pendet.jpg, February, March 2021.

[13] Rice Terraces at Jatiluwih. *Source*: Imacim, 2018, accessed via Wikimedia Commons, https://commons.wikimedia.org/wiki/File:Jatiluwih_rice_terraces.jpg, February, March 2021.

Made in the USA
Columbia, SC
18 March 2024

33253928R00068